Also by Matthew Silverman:

Baseball: The Biographical Encyclopedia (lead editor)
Big League Ballparks (coeditor)
Cubs by the Numbers (with Al Yellon and Kasey Ignarski)
The ESPN Baseball Encyclopedia (associate editor)
The ESPN Pro Football Encyclopedia (managing editor)
Mets by the Numbers (with Jon Springer)
Mets Essential
The Miracle Has Landed (coeditor)
New York Mets: The Complete Illustrated History
100 Things Mets Fans Should Know and Do Before They Die
Red Sox by the Numbers (with Bill Nowlin)
Shea Goodbye (with Keith Hernandez)
Ted Williams: My Life in Pictures (editor)
Total Baseball (managing editor)
Total Football (managing editor)
Ultimate Red Sox Companion (managing editor)

BASEBALL MISCELLANY

EVERYTHING YOU ALWAYS WANTED TO
KNOW ABOUT BASEBALL

MATTHEW SILVERMAN

Skyhorse Publishing

Skyhorse Publishing books may be purchased in bulk at special discounts for sales promotion, corporate gifts, fund-raising, or educational purposes. Special editions can also be created to specifications. For details, contact the Special Sales Department, Skyhorse Publishing, 307 West 36th Street, 11th Floor, New York, NY 10018 or info@skyhorsepublishing.com.

www.skyhorsepublishing.com

10 9 8 7 6 5 4 3 2 1

Photo credits for full page photos: Shutterstock Images, pages viii, xii, 24, 29, 42, 109, 154, 167; Dan Carubia, pages 1, 98, 161; Bill Nowlin, page 7; and the National Baseball Hall of Fame and Library, pages 13, 103, 122, 141, 147. Others taken by author.

Library of Congress Cataloging-in-Publication Data is available on file.
ISBN: 978-1-61608-196-6

Printed in China

For those who ignore the question "why baseball?" and watch and thrill and learn as the game rolls on.

CONTENTS

INTRODUCTION

From the first time a group of boys began playing an ancestral version of baseball, the game has looked pretty easy from afar. Throw ball, hit ball, catch ball, run! The game has always belonged to those who can master these skills. The stands are filled with those who only mastered them in theory or never made it in practice.

Baseball history goes back as far as you are willing to chase it. Bat and ball games have been documented back some 3,500 years ago to ancient Egypt. The game can be traced to eighteenth century New England or to a cow pasture in Cooperstown, New York, for those who like their baseball tales told tall. Wherever you want to say baseball began, it is forever moving back toward home, and every game is both utterly different and remarkably the same.

Baseball Miscellany selects twenty-seven fundamental questions about the game—as many questions as there are outs required for a nine-inning win. Since baseball is a series of unique moments ever reminiscent of previous events, some information is repeated. Corralling this information was as challenging as tracking down a deep drive on the dead run in center field with the wall approaching.

Baseball requires skill and strength plus the heart of a poet. In *Shoeless Joe*, author W. P. Kinsella sums up baseball's pull with a speech by a fictionalized version of J. D. Salinger—the character's name was changed to Terence Mann (played by James Earl Jones) in the film version, *Field of Dreams*:

I don't have to tell you that the one constant through all the years has been baseball. America has been erased like a blackboard, only to be rebuilt and then erased again. But baseball has marked time while America has rolled by like a procession of steamrollers.

I don't have to tell you that I made up the questions, but the answers belong to a lot of different people who provided information for the responses. First, thanks, as always, to my editor, Mark

Weinstein, and my agent, Anne Marie O'Farrell. Special appreciation goes to John Thorn, Paul Lukas, and former pitcher Jerry Reuss, the renowned southpaw, who also contributed his photographs to the book. Photo help was provided by Tim Wiles, John Horne, Freddy Berowski, Pat Kelly, and Bill Francis from the National Baseball Hall of Fame Library. Kudos for last-minute help from Al Yellon, Tim Donovan, Dan Sullivan, Joe LeMar, plus Bill and Liam Butler. Michael Guilbault. Heartfelt thanks for the photography of Dan Carubia and Bill Nowlin. Photos not credited belong to the author, who can be contacted at metsilverman.com.

As for written sources, here's a quick roster of Web sites: Athleticscholarships.net, Baseball Almanac, Baseball Fever, Baseball-Reference, Boston Sports Then and Now, ESPN, the Free Library, *Inside Science*, Jock Bio, LA84 Foundation, Louisville Slugger, Major League Baseball, Mental Floss, *Michigan Daily*, NASA, *New York Times*, *Nine*, SABR's Bio Project, San Francisco Museum, Science20.com, Seamheads.com, *Sports Illustrated*, Suite 101, UCLA, *USA Today*, and the *Wall Street Journal*.

And where would we be without baseball books? Notably *Baseball Before We Knew It* by David Block, *Crazy '08* by Cait Murphy, *Joe DiMaggio: The Hero's Life* by Richard Ben Cramer, *The ESPN Baseball Encyclopedia* by Gary Gillette and Pete Palmer, *The Neyer/James Guide to Pitchers* by Bill James and Rob Neyer, *Now Batting Number . . .* by Jack Looney, *Red Sox Threads* by Bill Nowlin, *Total Baseball* by John Thorn, et al., *Whatever Happened to the Hall of Fame* by Bill James, *Why a Curveball Curves* by *Popular Mechanics* (edited by Frank Vizard), *Wrigley Field: The Unauthorized Biography*, by Stuart Shea, and especially *The Dickson Baseball Dictionary* by Paul Dickson.

Now batter up.

WHY DOES THE VISITING TEAM ALWAYS BAT FIRST?

Go to any baseball game, be it Little League, Pony League, International League, or American League, and the team stepping up to the plate first is the visiting team. Asking *which* team is in the field as a game starts is one of those questions that anyone knowing anything about baseball would not ask. *Why* does the visiting team bat first? Well, that's a good question.

It is seen as a tactical advantage for a team to have "last licks"—the chance to score in the bottom of the final inning and not have to defend in the field if they take the lead. The same is true if the game goes extra innings. Records show that the home team has about a 51 percent chance of winning in extra innings—compared with 54 percent in regulation. Still, the idea that the home team could win at any moment in "bonus time" has kept many people in their seats even after beer and hot dog sales have been shut off at the ballyard.

Yet it has not always been this way. Visiting teams have not always batted first and have enjoyed this home-field advantage even while wearing the visiting gray. The home team long held the option to bat first or second. If there hadn't been a formal rule put in the books in the 1950s, one gets the feeling that Tony LaRussa's teams would bat first at home . . . with the pitcher hitting eighth.

Back in the day, LaRussa might have had a point. Before 1920 only a handful of baseballs—and sometimes just a single ball—made it into a pitcher's hand over the course of a game. (The death of Cleveland's Ray Chapman after being hit in the head by a pitch from Yankee Carl Mays on August 16 of that year led to umpires being instructed to put new balls—which are whiter and thus easier for the batter to see—into play more often.)

When fewer balls were used, the team leading off had the first chance to hit with the new ball. If that team had the lead, it had the benefit of a completely darkened and beat-up ball to pitch with by the time the last of the ninth inning came around.

Though sometimes the home team batted first more for promotional than strategic considerations, the reason why two American

Around the Horn

Around the horn has two meanings, though both describe whipping the ball quickly around the infield. There is the around the horn double play, from third baseman to second baseman to first baseman (5–4–3 for those scoring at home). The other around the horn is more relaxed, though it also involves sharp throws; the ball is thrown around the horn after the first or second out if nobody is on base (the shortstop is usually included in the latter version and the first baseman is left out, presumably because he handles the ball more frequently and doesn't need the mid-inning practice). The term refers to sailors going around the tip of South America at Cape Horn to travel from the Atlantic to the Pacific. Because of quickly arising storms, it was an often perilous journey; travel between the two oceans became far safer—and shorter—with the opening of the Panama Canal in 1914.

League home teams opened the 1903 season as visitors has been lost to time. The Washington Senators led off at home in the first game played by the team now known as the New York Yankees (who had just relocated from Baltimore). Ironically, visiting New York, then known as the Highlanders, scored first while batting second, yet they did not cross the plate again versus Al Orth, who earned the 3–1 win over Jack Chesbro. That same day, the St. Louis Browns batted first against the Chicago White Sox in chilly St. Louis. It didn't do much for the home club as Chicago romped, 14–4. The next day both the Senators and Browns reverted to type and let the visiting team bat first; in both cases the visiting team won. The Senators and Browns are probably not great examples of strategy since they both finished far off the pace in 1903.

For a more recent example, look no further than June 25–27, 2010, to an interleague series between the Toronto Blue Jays and Philadelphia Phillies. Originally scheduled for Toronto, it was moved to Citizens Bank Ballpark in Philly because of the G-20 Summit in Toronto, the fourth meeting of the Group of 20 (finance ministers and central bank governors from nineteen countries plus the European Union). With more than 11,000 uniformed police officers, security, and military personnel on duty in Toronto—a total higher than the attendance at eight Blue Jays home games at the Rogers Centre in 2010—authorities decided it best if the Jays made themselves scarce that weekend rather than create even more areas to monitor. The games could have been relocated to any number of neutral sites (the New York Mets and Florida Marlins, for example, would play

The first time the Arizona Diamondbacks got to bat first—or wear road grays—was in Los Angeles on April 7, 1998. Clad in white at home, the Dodgers and the battery of Chan Ho Park and Mike Piazza were unkind hosts in a 9-1 victory.

PHOTO CREDIT: JERRY REUSS

Baseball Miscellany

three games the following week in San Juan to further enthusiasm for the game in Puerto Rico). The Blue Jays, however, opted to give the weekend games to Philadelphia instead, where they would likely sell out and the Blue Jays would enjoy a nice slice of revenue.

The Blue Jays took the field first in Philadelphia with the Phillies batting first in road gray. The designated hitter was used—the first regular-season game in a National League park to utilize the DH (the 1984 World Series in San Diego marked the last time it happened at an NL park at all). It was very much like a game in Toronto, save for the 44,000 people hoping the Blue Jays would lose. The Blue Jays obliged, losing two out of three in their home away from home. Roy Halladay, Toronto's marquee player before being traded to Philly the previous winter, blanked his former team in seven innings in his first game as a "visitor" against Toronto. Wink, wink.

And Philadelphia finally got people to call the home team the Blue Jays. Back in the 1940s, new Phillies ownership attempted to change their name of the team to the Blue Jays, but it didn't stick. This G-20/2010 scheme took that wish just a bit too far.

Now what do scientists have to say of the batting last debate? The April 2010 issue of the magazine *Inside Science* took on the idea of an advantage for team's batting last: "In most games in which participants take turns, such as bowling or horseshoes, there's an advantage to going last. In baseball, the pitcher and the defense both have numerous strategic choices that affect the other's success, whereas in horseshoes, no one's trying to catch the final throw."

Theodore Turocy, a baseball fan and economist specializing in game theory summed it for laymen fans everywhere: "I don't think that has anything to do with batting last. It has everything to do with being at home."

QUOTABLE

For Starters

"Say this much for big league baseball—it is beyond question the greatest conversation piece ever invented in America."
—Bruce Catton, writer

HOW DOES A
CURVEBALL CURVE?

There has been enough research on the curving of a curveball that you'd think scientists should get scolded for spending so much time on baseball. But science, technology, and persistence have proven that a curveball does indeed curve . . . though some in the scientific community still contend that the way the ball is viewed makes the break on a curve seem larger than it is.

Testimony that a curveball curves can be acquired from any batter at any level of the game whose career was cut short by an inability to hit the hook, a line that stretches back to when the pitch was invented by Candy Cummings—some say Fred Goldsmith—in the late 1860s (or early 1870s, depending on which pitcher you favor as originator).

There's never been a doubt in the mind of pitchers as to whether a curve curves. Dizzy Dean, the National League's last 30-game winner (in 1934), summed it up best: "Stand behind a tree 60 feet away, and I'll whomp you with an optical illusion!" When asked his opinion, Jerry Reuss, who won 220 games over four decades (1969–1990) took a more down-to-business approach: "As a player, I didn't concern myself with the physics behind a curve . . . that was above my pay grade. I was concerned with grip, finger position and, most important, location."

Scientists, on the other hand, have been concerned with balls curving since before baseball existed. One of the greatest scientific minds of all, Isaac Newton, pondered the properties of a ball after it was struck in the popular seventeenth century game of

Tim Lincecum of the 2010 World Champion San Francisco Giants has one of the better curves in the game.

PHOTO CREDIT: SHUTTERSTOCK IMAGES

tennis. The Bernoulli Principle, named for eighteenth century mathematician Daniel Bernoulli, has been applied to how an airplane stays aloft as well as how a knee-buckling curve can fall in or out of the strike zone at the last instant.

So let's take Bernoulli out to the ballgame. A pitcher puts force on one side of the baseball to generate topspin. That creates an area of low pressure on the side of the ball with no force on it. The low pressure area makes the ball spin faster on that side. So a ball that looks like it is sailing wide of the plate tails back in and catches the corner. Stee-rike!

Popular Mechanics wrote the book on the subject, literally: *Why a Curveball Curves* from Hearst Books in 2008. Those mechanics credited the work of nineteenth century German physicist Gustav Magnus, who never threw a curve but hurled a neat theory on the subject. As *Popular Mechanics* summarized, "The effect is to generate a pressure difference across the ball, creating a lateral force component

How's that for an illusion? Jerry Reuss breaks off a big bender for the Cardinals in 1971.

Backdoor Slider

A backdoor slider is a slider that moves in the opposite direction of a traditional slider. A slider thrown by a right-handed pitcher should move to the outside corner for a left-handed batter, but a backdoor slider will seem to be headed to the outside only to cross the plate on the inside. Its late unexpected movement often results in strikes and outs—or at least gives the hitter something to think about.

that pushes the ball sideways. This lateral force, at right angles to the forward motion of the ball, is known as Magnus force."

In the late 1940s, with the discovery of the atom bomb and world tyranny taken care of, scientists could again turn to the important question of whether a curve really did curve. Aeronautics engineer Ralph B. Lightfoot used a wind tunnel and high-speed photography at the behest of his employer, Sikorsky Aircraft, to show that the curveball was real, though his findings were not published in a scientific journal. The debate continued.

Even NASA, which knows a thing or two about air currents against objects, has weighed in on the subject. The National Aeronautics and Space Administration points out on its Web site that the amount of force generated by a spinning ball depends on the amount of spin, the velocity of the ball, the size of the ball, and the density of the air. Taking the surroundings into account explains why a ball does not move as much in Denver's mile-high elevation. The Colorado Rockies installed a humidor in 2002 to prevent the baseballs from becoming drier and harder than balls at sea level. The humidor and the semblance of normalcy it brought to Coors Field baseball was a boon for all who ply the pitching trade.

To throw a curveball, start with these materials. Add arm.

PHOTO CREDIT: SHUTTERSTOCK IMAGES

Shifting from the physics lab to the operating table, be warned that the arm movement involved in throwing a curveball can harm developing arms. Some experts say the pitch should not be tried until age 16. Little League Baseball takes care of that by claiming research on the pitch is "inconclusive" and calling the curveballs thrown by the 12-year-olds in its nationally televised tournament "breaking balls." Now that's quite a curve.

The Big Curve

"The story of the curve ball is the story of the game itself. Some would say, of life itself." — Martin Quigley, writer

WHY WAS JOE DiMAGGIO CALLED "THE YANKEE CLIPPER"?

J oe DiMaggio had no shortage of success or nicknames during his fabled career with the New York Yankees.

Because it was a time where ribbing based on ancestry was a given, DiMaggio was called Dago when he got to the Yankees in 1936—the plethora of Italian American Yankees resulted in veterans Frank Crosetti and Tony Lazzeri having "Big" and "Little" stuck in front of the same nickname. Italians all across the world—plus a plucky yet unlucky Cuban fisherman in Ernest Hemingway's *The Old Man and the Sea*—would pass down their affection for the Yankees through generations. Playing off that ancestry, newspapers called DiMaggio The Roamin' Roman and Wallopin' Wop. There was Little Bambino (a tribute to his Ruth-like prowess and an allusion to the man he essentially replaced) and Big Giuseppe (even though he was technically Giuseppe Jr.). And everyone remembers the famous nickname Joltin' Joe, not to mention the simpler DiMag or Joe D. Mr. Coffee even entered the lineup when he served as pitchman for his beverage maker of choice.

But no name seemed to capture the imagination like the one bestowed on him in 1939. Richard Ben Cramer, author of *Joe DiMaggio: The Hero's Life*, pinpointed the creation of the name to an Arch McDonald broadcast: "Batting cleanup, Joe DiMaggio—the Yankee Clipper." Pan American airlines was calling its long, sleek airplanes "clippers," a name that conjured up images of a nine-teenth century clipper ship sailing majestically and swiftly across a sun-dappled bay on a crystal clear morning. The same kind of image that DiMaggio invoked as he gracefully roamed the massive outfield at Yankee Stadium, effortlessly tracking down long drives with seeming ease.

The name Yankee Clipper created images of swift vessels of sea and air, but a fishing boat was more appropriate for DiMaggio. Fisherman Giuseppe Paolo DiMaggio Sr. left Sicily in 1898 and settled in Martinez, California. He later moved to San Francisco's Fisherman's Wharf and had nine children, enough for a baseball team. The three youngest indeed grew up to play in the major leagues: Vince, Joe Jr.,

Did You Know?

One More Time
Since the modern World Series started in 1903, the longest period without a repeat world champion has been fourteen years. After the New York Yankees won consecutive World Series in 1977–78, it wasn't until the 1992–93 Toronto Blue Jays that a champion repeated. The 1980s marked the first decade without a repeat world champion. The Yankees and Oakland A's are the only teams to win at least three consecutive world championships.

Repeat Champs	Years
Chicago Cubs	1907–08
Boston Red Sox	1914–15
New York Giants	1921–22
New York Yankees	1927–28
Philadelphia Athletics	1929–30
New York Yankees	1936–39
New York Yankees	1949–53
New York Yankees	1961–62
Oakland A's	1972–74
New York Yankees	1977–78
Toronto Blue Jays	1992–93
New York Yankees	1998–2000

and Dom. Their father didn't want any of them playing baseball—"Too many shoes, too many pants," he complained—but when San Francisco mayor Angelo Rossi halted a game at Seals Stadium in

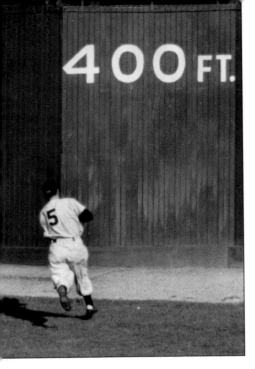

Joe DiMaggio shows clipper-esque grace hauling in a drive in deep center field.

front of a packed house to run out and shake Joe's hand after the teenager broke the Pacific Coast League record by getting a hit in his 49th straight game (DiMaggio would eventually hit in 61 straight for the San Francisco Seals), the parents DiMaggio were suddenly on board with this baseball thing.

A knee injury in 1934 put his sale to the Yankees on an installment plan. The Seals received $25,000 in Depression-era dollars plus five players and they got to keep their box office draw an extra year while he healed. And DiMaggio wasn't yet 20.

By the start of 1936 the Yankees had not won a pennant in three years—a seeming lifetime in the Bronx—but they won four straight world championships upon DiMaggio's arrival. In 1941 he set the all-time major league mark by hitting in 56 consecutive games amid

QUOTABLE

Lefty's Velocity Philosophy

"I'm throwing twice as hard as I ever did. The ball's just not getting there as fast." —Lefty Gomez, Hall of Fame pitcher

The *Gazela Primeiro*, which still sails out of Philadelphia, is similar to the nineteenth century clipper ships that got their name because they moved swiftly across trade routes. The Yankee Clipper conjured similar images of speed and grace.

PHOTO CREDIT: KARYL WEBER

a national fixation and was forever branded "Joltin' Joe" in the press and in song (sung by Betty Bonney with Les Brown and the Band of Renown). The Yankees won six pennants in DiMaggio's first seven years before he joined the Army in World War II. The two-time AL MVP spent three years in the military. He was kept away from combat, but he made plenty of public appearances and played lots of baseball. He returned to New York and had his worst year in the majors to that point in 1946: .290 average, 25 HRs, 95 RBIs (which gives an indication of how good those pre-war seasons were).

In 1947 he won his third MVP despite hitting five fewer home runs and driving in just two more runs (though he upped his average to .315). Most importantly, the Yankees won their sixth title with DiMaggio that year. The following year he led the league with 39 home runs—no easy feat hitting in the truly cavernous original Yankee Stadium—and knocked in 155. A heel operation in 1949 cost him half the season, but the Yankees overtook the Red Sox the final weekend and won the championship, as they would the next two years as well.

Baltimore Chop

No, it's not a delicacy at a fancy Maryland steakhouse, but rather it's a ball hit on or near home plate and bounces so high that the fielder has no play. When executed perfectly it can produce a nice little hit that usually travels less than 90 feet and perhaps goes that high in the air. Also simply called a chopper, the Baltimore variety got its name from the 1890s National League Baltimore Orioles of John McGraw, Wee Willie Keeler, and Wilbert Robinson, who perfected the technique with the help of a specially prepared home plate area by the groundskeeper. Choppers today invariably occur accidentally, but a close approximation of the old Orioles' method is demonstrated when a ball is chopped near the plate on artificial turf.

He called it quits after the 1951 season at age 36, not having played enough to threaten any all-time career records, though his 2-to-1 lifetime walk-to-strikeout ratio spoke of his batting eye and skill. A high strikeout total for him (36) and low home run output (12) in his final year kept him from finishing with more career homers (361) than strikeouts (369). Moreover, out of the ten World Series in his thirteen seasons in the majors, the Yankees lost only once in October.

DiMaggio had a boat named *The Yankee Clipper* in San Francisco. He and Marilyn Monroe could be spied fishing off it in the mornings after their marriage in 1954. The marriage lasted just nine months before they separated, but the Yankee Clipper name continued sailing long after his death in 1999 and still is instantly recognizable more than a century after the DiMaggios first chartered American waters.

WHY IS THE NEXT
BATTER CONSIDERED
TO BE "ON DECK"?

The term "on deck" is where baseball meets the sea. It was in coastal Maine where the first recorded use of on deck was used. And it was the only consolation of a long day on the ballfield.

Though there are sources that claim the term was used earlier in baseball in the 1860s, the popular usage of the term can be traced to the afternoon of August 6, 1872, when Boston's dominant National Association club, on a tour of Maine, came to Belfast to face the local nine, the Pastimes. The scorers from both teams were instructed to call out each hitter as they stepped up to the plate and note which batters were to follow in the lineup. Boston's scorer simply announced, "G. Wright at bat; Leonard and Barnes next." The Pastimes were no match for Boston on the field, losing 35–1, but Belfast blew them away when it came to public address duties. The Pastimes scorer made his announcements in a nautical fashion: "Moody at bat, Boardman on deck, Dinsmore in the hold."

To be on deck was to be on the main deck of a ship. Being in the hold was to be below deck, an image reinforced by a dugout or shaded area where teams waited their turn at bat. The Boston scorer liked this nautical bent so much that he took it for his own. Given that the Boston Red Stockings, forerunners of the Braves, took part in numerous exhibitions similar to the game in Belfast, there was ample opportunity for the terms to spread quickly. And given that Boston won 39 of 47 league games that year, and everybody likes a winner, the saying took hold. In the hold, however, became in the hole, though Joanna Carver Colcord's book, *Sea Language Comes Ashore*, states that the accepted nautical pronunciation of hold was hole.

So how did something that happened so long ago in a small town in Maine with an 1870s population of 5,300 still have a place in baseball's everyday jargon? The *Sporting News* received a letter in 1938 from a man in his nineties named Robert P. Chase giving the particulars of that day's events. How did he know? According to research into the story by Paul Dickson for his *Baseball Dictionary*, the Belfast newspaper account of the 1872 game reported that the pitcher who'd been hammered by Boston was named "Chase." The only man listed in the city directory by that name would have been 25 at the time. *The Sporting News* apparently got the story direct from the horse's mouth. Several decades after the fact, the story of the origin of the expression got back to Belfast when Jay Davis, the editor of the local paper, saw a story on the origin of the term in an Astrodome scorecard while on vacation in Texas. What goes around comes back around on deck.

Hall of Fame pitcher Tom Seaver waits on deck at Shea Stadium in 1983.

Banjo Hitter

A banjo hitter is a ballplayer with little power. The appalling number of home runs by confirmed banjo hitters in 1987 alerted baseball followers that "The Year of the Home Run" had officially arrived. As for the term, Baseball-reference.com theorized that it might have come from the sound of a "short hit coming off the bat, as being like the sound of a banjo, whereas a long hit would have made a different sound." Cue up the dueling banjos from the theme to *Deliverance*.

QUOTABLE

Reading Back to Front

"I always turn to the sports pages first, which record people's accomplishments. The front page has nothing but man's failures."—Earl Warren, chief justice of the United States (1953–69)

The retired deck circle from Pittsburgh's Forbes Field remains on duty at the Hall of Fame.

WHEN DID UMPIRES START USING HAND SIGNALS?

I t seems hard today to imagine a game without an umpire making some kind of sign with his hand to call a strike. Or pumping out a runner on a close play. Or spreading his wings like a bird to indicate the runner beat the tag. But in the early days of baseball you had to be right in the heat of the action to hear the call. If you were far off in the stands, or even playing the outfield, you had to read the runner's or fielder's body language to figure out how a close play was called.

That had to be frustrating, but imagine if you were standing right next to the umpire and could not hear the call. Rookie outfielder William Ellsworth Hoy knew the feeling all too well. He was deaf.

It being a crueler time, everyone called him "Dummy" despite Hoy serving as valedictorian at the Ohio School for the Deaf. Hoy, who'd lost his hearing at age three due to meningitis, operated a shoe repair shop in his native Hockstown, Ohio. He played baseball for the town team and was good enough to earn a contract with Oshkosh of the Northwest League in 1886.

Not being able to hear the umpire's calls, he constantly had to look to his third-base coach to see if a strike or a ball had been called,

BILL McGOWAN'S SCHOOL for UMPIRES
COCOA — 1949 — FLORIDA

Bill McGowan's School for UMPIRES trains the 1949 ump crop in Cocoa, Florida.
PHOTO CREDIT: NATIONAL BASEBALL HALL OF FAME, COOPERSTOWN, NY

When did umpires start using hand signals? | 25

Did You Know?

Drinking Game

The "Beer and Whiskey League" was not a collection of hard-drinking slow-pitch softball teams in some Rust Belt city, it was a successful major league in the nineteenth century . . . located in several Rust Belt cities. The American Association was the first rival of the National League and competitor in a nineteenth century version of the "World Series," with the NL holding a 4–1–2 edge (the St. Louis Brown Stockings, predecessor of today's Cardinals, were the only AA squad to defeat the NL). The league earned its bibulous nickname for selling alcohol in its parks, with four of its owners not so incidentally involved in breweries or distilleries. The Cincinnati Reds had left the NL in 1880 after refusing to cease Sunday play and alcohol sales at their park (Sunday was the day most workers had off and Cincinnati's large German population liked to take a drink at a ballgame). The American Association also charged a 25-cent admission, half what the NL asked. The AA drew well and turned a profit, eventually leading the NL to form an agreement to play a postseason championship "World Series"—and agree to the reserve clause for players. The AA lasted longer than any other National League rival until the American League's emergence in 1901.

and opponents tried to quick pitch him. The coach quickly relayed hand signals and Hoy went from batting .219 as a rookie at Oshkosh to .367 his second season—and to the National League the year after

William "Dummy" Hoy, the supposed inspiration for the umpire hand signal, poses for a baseball card found in a pack of nineteenth century cigarettes.
PHOTO CREDIT: NATIONAL BASEBALL HALL OF FAME LIBRARY, COOPERSTOWN, NY

that. His speed and ability to read a pitcher's movements allowed him to steal 82 bases for Washington, the highest total by a rookie until Vince Coleman had 110 thefts for St. Louis in 1985. During Hoy's time, however, runners were credited with a steal for taking an extra base on a hit or an out, so it is difficult to compare his steal totals with modern players. But Hoy did have a superb eye (drawing 1,006 bases on balls) and arm (he had seven seasons with more than 20 assists from center field). He surpassed 100 runs nine times, and amassed 2,048 hits. In his final year in 1902 he faced New York Giants rookie Dummy Taylor, also deaf and likewise stuck with the unbecoming nickname. There has never been another major league confrontation between deaf pitcher and batter.

Hoy's part in the birth of umpire hand signals is inspirational, but it is also hard to prove. Hoy lived to be 99, throwing out the first pitch during the 1961 World Series, two months before his death. But during his long life, no one credited Hoy with helping create umpire hand signals. Turn-of-the-century umps Cy Rigler and Bill Klem are recognized for popularizing hand signals so that outfielders—plus the paying customers—had an idea of what was going on at the plate. Klem's plaque in the Hall of Fame even claims, "Credited with introducing arm signals indicating strikes and fair or foul balls." *Signs*, a 2010 documentary on the origin of umpire hand signals, notes that the source for that credit came from Klem himself.

Hot Stove

"People ask me what I do in winter when there's no baseball. I'll tell you what I do. I stare out the window and wait for spring." — Rogers Hornsby, Hall of Fame second baseman

Don Casper, director and co-producer of *Signs*, admits, "The truth is a little gray." It often is, in baseball and in life. Like many of the great questions that hover around baseball, the origin of umpire hand signals comes with a great story . . . and another theory that seems to disprove it. Sometimes you just wish there was one call and that was it. And in this case they'd certainly use hand signals.

BASEBALL DEFINED

Blooper

A blooper is the lifeblood of hitters and the bane of pitchers. It is a fly ball, usually softly hit, that lands between the infield and outfield for a hit. Pitcher Jim Brosnan, author of 1960 book, *The Long Season*, proclaimed the name came from the sound made when bats hits ball on such a hit: "A soft tomato struck by a broomstick." It has also been popularly known as a Texas Leaguer—a name that dates to the nineteenth century—but more recent names that stand in for such a hit include banjo hit, dink hit, dunker, flare, gorker, lollipop, looper, parachute hit, and pooper.

WHY DO SOME NEW STADIUMS HAVE THE SAME NAMES AS OLD ONES?

Baseball is all about tradition. And in the twenty-first century, tradition sells. That is why when Yankee Stadium opened in 2009, technically the third incarnation of the stadium built in 1923 and rebuilt on the same spot in 1976, it kept the name despite moving several hundred yards away in the same Bronx neighborhood. The Yankees resisted selling the name to a corporation or changing it to something else traditional yet distinctive, such as Babe Ruth Stadium (the original house *was* built on the Bambino's popularity in the 1920s). The death of George Steinbrenner in 2010 raised the remote possibility the stadium could be renamed for him, though the stadium for the Class A Tampa Yankees, also the team's spring training home, is already named after the late Yankees owner.

The Yankees are a brand name and it suits the franchise to retain the name for the stadium. And keeping it Yankee Stadium maintains the option that the team can still have a payday someday by selling the rights, though the team has stated no plans to do so.

Keeping the same stadium name after moving to a new location dates back long before naming right fees were the norm. When stadiums were made out of wood in the nineteenth century, fire was often the reason a new ballpark was constructed, though many of these hastily built structures became rundown or the team moved to a better location and simply kept the old ballpark name.

Boston's South End Grounds was the first ballpark moniker to have multiple lives at different addresses. According to the *ESPN Baseball Encyclopedia*, South End Grounds had three incarnations for the Boston Braves between 1871 and 1914. Three Washington Parks in Brooklyn were home to teams in three major leagues: the Atlantics of the American Association, the Bridegrooms (later called the Dodgers) of the National League, and finally the Tip-Tops of the Federal League in 1914–15. Pittsburgh's Exposition Park had two incarnations in the 1880s, as did the Baker Bowl in Philadelphia (one erected in 1887 and a more permanent structure in 1895). The Washington Senators had two American League Parks from 1901–10, though their second version was called National Park by some, sounding a lot like the home of the city's current team: Nationals Park.

In Chicago, the first South Side Park housed the 1891–93 Cubs and the second was home to the White Sox, beginning with the first year of the American League club's existence in 1901. Charlie Comiskey built a beautiful ballpark for his White Sox in 1910 and named it after himself. A new stadium was built in the lot next to the old park in 1991 and called new Comiskey, which had a far nicer ring than U.S. Cellar Field, dialed in in 2003.

Before St. Louis went through three Busch Stadiums, it had two Sportsman's Parks. The first Sportsman's Park housed the team now known as the Cardinals, then an American Association team called the Brown Stockings, from 1882–91. The Milwaukee Brewers moved to St. Louis following the American League's inaugural season, adopted the name Browns, and erected a new Sportsman's Park in 1902. The Cardinals came in as tenants in 1920 and took over the place shortly before the Browns relocated to Baltimore in 1953. The brewing Busch family bought the Cardinals and the ballpark, originally wanting to name it Budweiser Stadium. The other owners deemed that too crass and commercial (which sounds funny today).

The third, and latest, incarnation of Busch Stadium.

So Augie Busch named the ballpark after himself and then christened a new beer called Busch. The name stuck through the building of a multi-use stadium in 1966 and the baseball-only park in 2006, each facility built in the same area near the Gateway Arch.

Yet no stadium has had as many incarnations as the Polo Grounds in New York. The grounds known by that name hosted the baseball Giants, the football Giants, the American Association champion Mets of 1884, the "Can't Anybody Here Play This Game" National League expansion Mets of 1962, the not Jet ready American Football League New York Titans, and the first Yankees team to claim a pennant—also the first sports team to draw a million fans in a season. Some still argue whether there were four or five different versions of the Manhattan ballpark. We'll just say there was plenty of Polo to go around.

Polo was the game played at 110th Street and Fifth Avenue, on a field directly across from the northeast entrance to Central Park. Baseball took over in the 1880s. After a semi-pro team called the Metropolitans played there initially, it served as home to both the NL Giants and the AA Mets with concurrent eastern and western fields (hence the controversy over the exact number incarnations). The original park was in the way of the city's plans for a new street grid and the Giants—after using a couple of temporary ballparks—moved uptown in July 1889 to 155th Street and Eighth Avenue, next to an elevated

Black Jack in the Tiger pen: Jack McDowell of the White Sox warms up at Tiger Stadium's bullpen in foul territory before a 1992 start in Detroit.

Did You Know?

Hot Diggety

Of the many innovations that baseball has brought society, perhaps its most universal is the hot dog. Harry Mosley Stevens had the turn of the century ice cream and soft drink concession for the New York Giants at the Polo Grounds. His wares sold poorly in cool temperatures early in the season, so he sought something with more appeal. He came up with serving wieners on a bun. Maybe he wasn't the first to serve up the dish, but Stevens popularized it to the point where a century later it's hard to picture a wiener served at a concessions stand any other way. Cartoonist Thomas Dorgan is credited with an illustration that shortened the "red hot dachshund sausages" to hot dog. Again, the name probably predated the efforts of Stevens or Dorgan—no such cartoon has ever been found—but it makes for a good story easily told while enjoying a hot dog at a ballgame. And the hot dog made Harry M. Stevens Inc. "The King of Sports Concessions"—though Stevens had gotten things off the ground in 1887 by reformatting the scorecard and making it a desirable item for fans and a profit point for himself. The company was the longest-running sports concessionaire, serving the Astrodome, Fenway Park, Shea Stadium, plus venues in other sports, when it was sold to Aramark in 1994.

Scott Linebrink (71) and fellow Milwaukee moundsmen settle in before an afternoon in the center field bullpen at Pittsburgh's PNC Park.

train terminus. The third incarnation of the Polo Grounds was originally termed Brotherhood Park for the short-lived Players' League. The NL club took over the structure by Coogan's Bluff in 1890 and the Giants made it New York's most famous outdoor sporting venue—rebuilding it in concrete and steel following a 1911 fire. The Polo Grounds was trumped, however, by Yankee Stadium in 1923, built after the Giants kicked out the tenant Yankees for having the nerve to outdraw them in their own park because of that Ruth character.

Casey's Little Secret

"The secret of managing is to keep the guys who hate you away from the guys who are undecided."—Casey Stengel, Hall of Fame manager

Bullpen

With the preponderance of relief pitching today, anyone who has paid attention to a game or two should know that the bullpen is the place from which fresh pitchers emerge. The pens are located either behind the outfield fences or along the foul lines, with one for the home club and another for the visitor. The question is: why is it called the bullpen? There are about as many theories as to how the bullpen got its name as there are relievers warming up in them. One hypothesis suggests it's because of the Bull Durham tobacco advertisements at many ballparks in the early 1900s. Because the large signs cast such a long shadow, pitchers liked to warm up in the shade of them during games. Or maybe the "bull" came from the mouths of the idle pitchers, so managers banished them to keep them from yapping on the bench during a game—a theory forwarded by Casey Stengel, who could sling the bull with anybody. Paul Dickson, who gathered a number of far-flung theories in his *Baseball Dictionary*, noted that Civil War prisoners were roped off like cattle and peacetime convicts continued the term. The baseball bullpen remains the place where starting pitchers are banished for falling out of effectiveness or favor.

WHY DO PITCHERS THROW OVERHAND IN BASEBALL AND UNDERHAND IN SOFTBALL?

Actually, baseball began with pitchers throwing underhand. In 1883 a rule was inserted to allow pitchers to deliver the baseball from shoulder height. The resulting effectiveness of pitching overhand ensured that no one would pitch traditional underhand again. There is no actual rule barring a professional baseball pitcher from throwing a baseball underhand, and there have been numerous submarine pitchers whose knuckles have practically scraped the mound when making their delivery.

Softball rules, on the other hand, state that pitchers must pitch underhand. Different leagues and levels have limits on how softball pitchers can deliver the ball to the plate. Some slow-pitch leagues insist on a certain pitching arc and a few fast-pitch circuits bar the powerful "windmill" windup to afford batters a better chance of contact.

At softball's highest collegiate, amateur, and professional levels, pitching dominates. The underhand motion and the smaller distance between plate and mound (43 feet for women and 46 feet for men) allow pitchers to throw far more frequently than in the more taxing overhand motion in baseball. But the game we know as softball origi-nated as a winter game—as a way of keeping ballplaying skills sharp during the off-season—and throwing underhand seemed the best way to make sure that arms stayed healthy.

Baseball was already popular enough in the late nineteenth century that ways were sought to play it all year long. People tried playing the game in the snow and on the ice, but that proved unsat-isfactory to most and, well, cold. So winter indoor baseball was created in Chicago in 1887, when a gym full of bored, sports-minded college students used a boxing glove as a ball, a broken-off broom handle as a bat, and drew bases on the floor in chalk. Note that this was four years before the invention of an entirely different indoor game to keep people occupied in the winter: basketball. Like James Naismith's game of basketball, softball also has an inventor, George Hancock—the gentleman who turned the broom into a bat and shouted "play ball."

Once the weather warmed up, the game moved out of the gymnasium and onto the field — using a ball instead of a boxing glove. Unlike baseball, which requires a certain level of skill to hit good pitching, this new — or, dare one say, softer — version of baseball made it much easier for novices or unskilled athletes to play and enjoy. Called indoor-outdoor by Hancock and kitten ball in Minneapolis, where a version of the same game developed independently, the Playground Society of America gave softball the seal of approval as a good game for children in 1910. Around that time a tenth player, or rover, was added for recreational play. (It's ironic that in a game where offense is the driving force, an extra fielder would be added.) The Depression made softball even more popular since it cost relatively little to play, kept a lot of people busy, and allowed someone down on his luck to take out his frustrations on a slow-moving ball.

The name softball, started at a Denver YMCA in the 1920s, is perplexing because the most commonly used ball is nearly as hard as a baseball and just about double the size. A softball is generally

Recreational softball is played by some 3.5 million players, according to the Amateur Softball Association. That's a lot of swings.

12 inches in circumference and weighs between 6 and 7 ounces; by comparison, the officials rules state that a baseball "shall weigh not less than five nor more than 5 ¼ ounces avoirdupois and measure not less than nine nor more than 9 ¼ inches in circumference." There are versions of softball played with balls as large as 16 inches around.

Both men and women started to develop softball competitively, with pitchers throwing harder as a result. For most boys and men, softball was often seen as a game to gravitate to as they grew older and baseball became either too difficult or was no longer available at an organized level. For girls and women, softball was the only game generally offered on the diamond (though girls would win the right to play Little League Baseball in 1974).

Joe LeMar of the Rollin' Red Six awaits a pitch in the National Wheelchair Softball Association championshp played at New York's Citi Field in 2010.

By 1943 *Time* magazine estimated there were 40,000 semi-pro women's softball teams in the United States. That year a select few were tapped to play in the All-American Girls Softball League, started by Chicago Cubs owner Philip K. Wrigley during World War II. It soon switched from underhand to overhand, with the softball exchanged for a hardball. The All-American Girls Professional Baseball League lasted until 1954. Almost four decades later the league got its due

QUOTABLE

Base Thief's Remorse

"When we played softball, I'd steal second base, feel guilty, and go back." — Woody Allen, director

when the Hall of Fame recognized the AAGPBL and Penny Marshall subsequently made a film about it, *A League of Their Own*.

Fast-pitch softball developed as an international game in the 1960s and the International Professional Women's Softball League began play in 1976, lasting four years. The growth of collegiate softball led to the development of the Women's College World Series in 1982. Two professional softball leagues came and went in the 1990s, though the idea was revived in 2004 as National Pro Fastpitch. (A professional women's baseball team, the Colorado Silver Bullets, lasted four seasons in the 1990s.)

Baseball and softball took a hit when the International Olympic Committee removed those sports from the Olympics starting in 2012, the first sports cut from the roster since polo got the ax after 1936. A heavy European presence and seeming anti-American sentiment on the committee doomed both sports, which had only been added to the Olympics in the 1990s (baseball in 1992, softball in 1996). The games will go on; the Games will be the poorer for the loss.

BASEBALL DEFINED

Butcher Boy

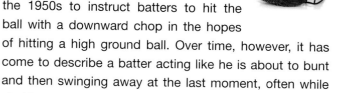

The term butcher boy was coined in the 1950s to instruct batters to hit the ball with a downward chop in the hopes of hitting a high ground ball. Over time, however, it has come to describe a batter acting like he is about to bunt and then swinging away at the last moment, often while choking up on the bat and taking advantage of the defense moving in on a bunt play. With few offensive weapons at their disposal, pitchers are generally most likely to try the butcher boy.

WHY DO TEAMS START A DIFFERENT PITCHER EACH DAY?

There was a time when the same pitcher threw just about every game. In 1876, the first year of the National League, Jim Devlin started and completed 68 of Louisville's 69 games. He won 30 and was still 17 victories behind the league leader, Chicago's Al Spalding—he of the future sporting goods empire.

These were the days of underhand pitching—and short pitching careers. The records for starts and complete games were set during this era by Cincinnati's Will White in 1879. (Pud Galvin would tie his starts mark in 1883.) In 1884 pitchers were permitted to throw overhand, which enabled them more speed yet at the same time put more stress on the arm. Teams still treated pitchers like pitching machines—if those had been invented yet. Old Hoss Radbourn of the NL champion Providence Grays put together the all-time record for wins that year with 59 in a 112-game schedule; his 678 2/3 innings were just four outs shy of White's five-year-old record. Radbourn's 22 innings in three games against the American Association's New York Metropolitans, the first such "World Series," would have pushed him past 700 innings, but even back then regular-season and post season numbers didn't mix.

By 1892 the schedule stood at 154 games. Most teams had by then moved to three rotating starters. Still, the "ace" sometimes pitched more frequently than once every three games. The work was distributed fairly by 1892 NL champion Boston, while the Giants and Chicago were the only teams whose aces tossed more than 50 complete games. Then the job got harder.

In 1893 the distance between the mound and home was changed from 55 feet to its current measure of 60 feet 6 inches, with pitchers required to keep their foot on a rubber plate. Even with the schedule trimmed by 22 games, the NL as a whole crossed home plate nearly 1,000 more times. The league batting average increased by 45 points and ERA jumped by 1.32 runs, with no team having an ERA below 4.00. In fact, St. Louis' ERA went from league-worst in 1892 at 4.20 to league-best a year later at 4.06. The Browns employed four starters for most of 1893, getting 40-plus starts apiece from Ted Breitenstein and Kid Gleason (later manager of the 1919 Black Sox), while Pink Hawley and Dad Clarkson split the remaining 45 starts.

Pitchers caught a break in 1894 when foul bunts were counted as strikes—previously batters could spoil pitches at will with bunts—though team batting averages reached epic proportions at .309 for the NL with Boston's Hugh Duffy recording an all-time high .440. St. Louis' Breitenstein turned into Frankenstein, allowing a record 497 hits and 320 runs, though he led the league in starts (50) and complete games (46). Flame-throwing Amos Rusie was the only pitcher with an ERA under 3.00; Rusie was one of five starters used by the Giants, though he and Jouett Meekin combined for 109 of those starts. The most consistent pitching star of that era was Cy Young, who started, won, and threw more innings than anybody ever will, yet he never led the major leagues in starts.

The new century brought the American League and high stakes competition for top pitching. For the first time, leaders in starts were generally making 40-plus instead of 50 or more. Then Jack Chesbro of the New York Highlanders broke the mold. In 1904, the first year the 154-game schedule was reinstated, Happy Jack started 51 games, completed 48, won 41, threw 454 2/3 innings, and faced 1,720 batters, all untouched American League records. New York had three semi-regular pitchers who *combined* to start 47 games, though 23-game winner Jack Powell was second to Chesbro with 47 games pitched. The next year Rube Waddell won the pitching Triple Crown and also led the AL in games, but Waddell had fewer starts and innings than Athletics teammate Eddie Plank. Manager Connie Mack had five pitchers throw 183 innings or more. When push came to shove, however, managers still rode their aces unremittingly. The Giants beat the A's in the World Series with John McGraw pitching Christy Mathewson three times in five days—Matty responded with a shutout in each start.

The advent of the World Series provides a study into how the best teams utilize their staffs in the most crucial games. While Pittsburgh manager Fred Clarke pitched Deacon Phillippe against Boston a record five times in the inaugural best-of-nine World Series in 1903, Clarke went with rookie Babe Adams—who was fifth on the team in wins—for three starts in 1909 as the Pirates beat the Tigers in seven games. Phillippe, still a Pirate, allowed no runs in six relief innings in 1909—remarkably, his arm hadn't fallen off.

Three starts by your ace became the standard procedure for years to come in the World Series, though there was plenty of room for experimentation. Detroit's Mayo Smith became the last manager to start two pitchers three times each in one World Series in 1968. It worked.

Managers were more inclined to ride their best arms than protect them as pitching dominated the landscape again. In 1972, the last year before the designated hitter, Chuck Tanner's White Sox had three pitchers make 40-plus starts; the rest of the staff started just 18 games. A change in philosophy commenced just five years later as free agency pushed up salaries not just for elite pitchers, but for reliable arms that could perform and avoid injury. Wayne Garland went from innings eater to money eater after the Indians lavished a 10-year contract on the pitcher after his only 20-win and 200-inning season.

Garland was far from the only well-compensated pitcher to get injured after reaching a payday in the early years of free agency. The average salary had gone up by less than $35,000 from 1966–1976; in the ensuing decade it increased by $350,000. Whereas managers had traditionally learned through trial and error which arms could best hold up, more and more caution crept into the decision making process. At the same time, more stress was put on the arms of relief pitchers. Other than ninth-inning closers, relievers are often the least expensive and most replaceable members of a team.

The five-man rotation became universal, which meant that even the best starters didn't reach 40 starts, save for knuckleballers like Phil Niekro and Charlie Hough. These war horses were the last pitchers in each league to reach the 40-start plateau. (Given the durability of knuckleballers, it is surprising more teams don't find ways to teach that pitch to more players.)

The last 300-inning season by a pitcher was more than 30 years ago (Steve Carlton, 1980). And 2000 was the last time each league had more than 100 complete games. The National League reached an all-time low with just 48 complete games in 2007, as three teams went without anyone tossing nine innings all year. The blind reliance on pitch counts without finding out which pitchers can best handle excess work has changed the game yet again in the 2000s. This tendency has placed a premium on strike throwers and on offenses able to wait out a starter, get him to surpass the magical 100-pitch threshold, and then attack his replacements. It sure is a long way from Jim Devlin, Al Spalding, and the one-man staff.

Due to pitch counts, innings limits, and the modern reliance on often unrelaible relievers, Randy Johnson could be the last 300-game winner for some time.

PHOTO CREDIT: JERRY REUSS

Did You Know?

Aces High

A pitching staff is hard pressed in a decade to duplicate what a yeoman starter could do in single year back in the day. Hard as it is to compare different eras, it is also kind of fun. Look at the Cubs, for example. Chicago's Bill Hutchinson had 67 complete games in 1892, still a game shy of John Clarkson's 1885 club record, yet that total exceeded the 64 complete games the Cubs accrued in the 11 seasons from 2000–2010. Break out the liniments for the pitching arm. Let's pitch two!

John Clarkson, whose career began when pitchers still threw underhand, won 328 games in a 12-year career in which he won 30 or more games six times, including 53 wins for Chicago in 1885.

Don't Dare Tell G About Pitch Counts

"Too many pitchers, that's all, there are just too many pitchers. Ten or twelve on a team. Don't see how any of them get enough work. Four starting pitchers and one relief man ought to be enough. Pitch 'em every three days and you'd find they'd get control and good, strong arms."

—Cy Young, Hall of Fame pitcher

BASEBALL DEFINED

Can of Corn

A can of corn is a high fly ball that is caught with minimum effort, generally by an outfielder. The term dates back to the late nineteenth century, when a storekeeper would use a stick to knock down a canned item from a high shelf and catch it effortlessly. That was as easy as a can of corn.

WHY IS THE NUMBER 42 ON THE WALL AT EVERY STADIUM?

This is one question, dear reader, to which we hope you already know the answer. Since a few major leaguers over the years have claimed ignorance as to the identity of number 42, however, it's not far-fetched to think some others might have missed it as well.

Number 42 took the field in Brooklyn the afternoon of April 15, 1947. It had been over a year since its wearer was signed by Dodgers president and general manager Branch Rickey and sent to the minor league Montreal Royals for a year of professional and personal seasoning. When he put on his glove and hit the diamond at Ebbets Field for the first time, Jackie Robinson became an American pioneer.

No African American had played in a major league game since 1884. Moses Fleetwood Walker played that year for Toledo Blue Stockings, which had just joined the American Association. A stand-out catcher on the first baseball team at Oberlin College in 1881, he was recruited to play for the University of Michigan (college rules of eligibility weren't quite as complicated then). He not only integrated Michigan sports, he helped the Wolverines win the first title in the Western Baseball League (predecessor to the Big Ten). The following year he turned professional, joining Toledo of the Northwest League and catching 60 games back when catchers wore no gloves or equipment. Naturally, Walker was part of the roster in 1884 when the Blue Stockings joined the American Association, major league competition for the National League.

Walker batted .263 while catching 41 games for Toledo. His brother Welday, who followed him to Michigan, briefly played for the Blue Stockings in 1884, becoming the second—and last—African American to play in the major leagues for 63 years. Cap Anson, player-manager of the National League's Chicago White Stockings (forerunners of the Cubs), insisted that he would cancel an exhibition against Toledo if Fleet Walker played. The Blue Stockings called Anson's bluff and the game was played. Later that season an anonymous letter threatened violence if Walker accompanied Toledo to play in Richmond, but Walker was already injured and did not travel with the team. Toledo did not return to the AA in 1885 as the league pared to eight teams. With Walker playing for Syracuse in the International League in 1889, Anson again threatened to cancel an exhibition if Walker and star pitcher George Stovey, also African American, took the field. This time his manager caved, setting a precedent that would carry over in every affiliated league until 1946, when Rickey signed Robinson.

Attitudes toward race had barely changed between the time Walker was forced off the field and Robinson forced his way onto it. Opponents, fans, and even some teammates were up in arms about Robinson breaking the color line. It was not just a sports color line he was breaking. Most institutions, from the U.S. military on down, had long traditions of segregation. While Robinson was a three-sport star at UCLA—his fourth sport was baseball, and he batted .097 in his only year on the team—away from campus he was just another black man. He served in the segregated Army and later joined the Negro League Kansas City Monarchs. His athletic skill and determined manner brought him to Rickey's attention.

Commissioner Albert "Happy" Chandler also pushed for Robinson's entry into the game. The former Kentucky governor had resigned his U.S. Senate seat in 1945 to succeed the deceased Kenesaw Mountain Landis, the game's first commissioner and vehement opponent to integrating the game—even in the face of severe manpower shortages during World War II. Every club opposed Robinson entering the majors save for Brooklyn, and his support for Robinson probably cost Chandler a second term as commissioner. Kentucky, however, voted him to a second term as governor.

Another Kentuckian, Pee Wee Reese, played one of the most important roles on the field. The team's shortstop and captain, Reese refused to sign a petition circulated by a few Dodgers of Southern descent to boycott if Robinson joined the team. With fans mercilessly heckling Robinson on his first road trip in Cincinnati, Reese stood close to Robinson with his arm on the rookie in a memorable display

Every time Jackie Robinson stepped onto a major league field, all eyes were on him.

of support. A sculpture of that moment was dedicated outside the ballpark for the Brooklyn Cyclones in 2005. "It came as such a relief to him," Rachel Robinson, Jackie's widow, said of Reese's gesture, "that a teammate and the captain of the team would go out of his way in such a public fashion to express friendship."

Robinson took out his frustrations on the field. His daring base-running and superb play helped the Dodgers win six pennants in his ten-year career. African Americans across the country became fans of the Dodgers, whose continued use of the pipeline from the

Negro Leagues to the major leagues helped fuel the club's resurgence. Negro League baseball, established by Rube Foster in 1920, provided a chance for blacks to play the game professionally for four decades. Though the shift of top African-American talent to the major leagues slowly killed off the Negro Leagues, some of the game's greatest stars had their first taste of professional ball in the Negro Leagues: Hank Aaron, Ernie Banks, Roy Campanella, Larry Doby, Monte Irvin, and Willie Mays, not to mention ageless Satchell Paige and dozens more who followed Jackie Robinson's path from segregated ball to the big leagues.

Robinson was baseball's first Rookie of the Year in 1947 and was batting champion plus league MVP in 1949. Not surprisingly, he was the first African American inducted in Cooperstown, opening

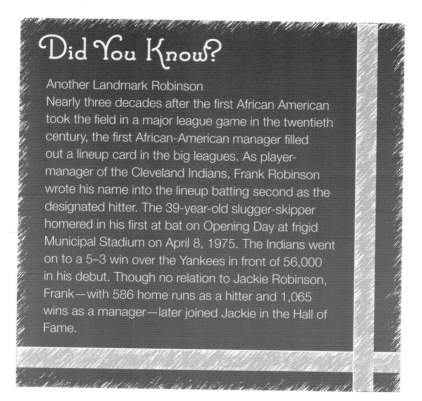

Did You Know?

Another Landmark Robinson
Nearly three decades after the first African American took the field in a major league game in the twentieth century, the first African-American manager filled out a lineup card in the big leagues. As player-manager of the Cleveland Indians, Frank Robinson wrote his name into the lineup batting second as the designated hitter. The 39-year-old slugger-skipper homered in his first at bat on Opening Day at frigid Municipal Stadium on April 8, 1975. The Indians went on to a 5–3 win over the Yankees in front of 56,000 in his debut. Though no relation to Jackie Robinson, Frank—with 586 home runs as a hitter and 1,065 wins as a manager—later joined Jackie in the Hall of Fame.

Frank Robinson, a Rookie of the Year, Triple Crown winner, and the only player to earn MVP in both leagues, became the first African American to manage a major league team with Cleveland in 1975.

the doors for all. He died in 1972 at age 53, three years shy of seeing the first African American manager.

The retirement of a player's number throughout baseball was another first in the game's history. At an event at Shea Stadium to mark the fiftieth anniversary of Robinson's landmark debut, commissioner Bud Selig upstaged President Bill Clinton by announcing that number 42 would be retired throughout organized baseball. Only players already issued the number at the time of the 1997 announcement could continue wearing it. A decade later, every player on every team began wearing number 42 on April 15 to honor one of the game's true heroes.

BASEBALL DEFINED

Cheese

Cheese is the fastball. It is also called cheddar, especially when it is hard to hit. Varieties include good cheese, hard cheese, and high cheese. Even if he can't hit the stuff, all this talk can make a person hungry.

Answering to a Higher Authority

"I'm going to have to meet my Maker some day. And if He asks me why I didn't let [Jackie Robinson] play, and I say it's because he's black, that might not be a satisfactory answer."
—Albert "Happy" Chandler, commissioner (1945–51)

Rachel Robinson, Jackie's widow, speaking at the 2008 "Character and Courage" ceremony at the Hall of Fame as statues of (from left) Lou Gehrig, Robinson, and Roberto Clemente are unveiled.

THE

SUBWAY SHOWDOWN

1997

YANKEES · METS

WHY IS THERE A
NATIONAL LEAGUE
AND AN AMERICAN
LEAGUE?

OFFICIAL

PUBLICATION

NEW YORK YANKEES VS

J ust as Coca-Cola has a rivalry with Pepsi, the National League and American League came to prominence as rivals. The idea of a rivalry between leagues sounds a bit preposterous today since Major League Baseball is now a single entity with no clear definition between AL and NL, except in the standings. Not long ago the leagues were quite different, with their own umpires, presidents, offices, and structure. The All-Star Game, once hotly contested because of league pride by the players, today is a watered-down exhibition that required the inducement of World Series home-field for the winning league to make it more appealing. Television ratings for the game continue to dwindle regardless.

There is, however, one major difference between the two leagues: the designated hitter. The American League has used the DH since 1973 while the NL has held firm to pitchers coming to bat. The DH was used in alternate years in the World Series from 1976 through 1984, which was probably more of an advantage to teams with the rule in their favor than having an extra home game (both the DH and home field alternated on a yearly basis). Since the 1985 World Series, the DH has been used in the AL park and the pitchers have batted in the NL park. This rule was adopted for interleague play starting in 1997. Yet the idea of the two leagues playing one another, or coexisting at all, was undreamed of at the dawn of the twentieth century.

Founded in 1876, the National League survived three other "major leagues" in its first 25 seasons. The American Association mostly coexisted with the NL for a decade (1882–1891) before folding, and two other leagues were pushed aside after one year: the Union Association in 1884 and the Players' League in 1890. By 1899 the National League bulged with a dozen teams and it consolidated power and talent by trimming four cities from its ranks: Baltimore, Cleveland, Louisville, and Washington. National League owners held a major league monopoly, not unlike many tycoons of the day who controlled the market by controlling the product. But there was another group of baseball men with eyes fixed on the big leagues and the big time.

Did You Know?

Accommodating Brewers

The Milwaukee Brewers are the only team in history to call four different divisions home. And that doesn't even take into account that Brewers was the name of an original American League franchise in 1901, but the club moved from Milwaukee to St. Louis in 1902 and became the Browns (and later relocated to Baltimore as the Orioles).

The current franchise known as the Brewers began life as the Seattle Pilots, a 1969 American League expansion team. The Pilots, of *Ball Four* fame, were the first team to finish last in the newly created AL West. The club abruptly moved the following spring to Milwaukee and became the Brewers, though maintaining a place in the AL West. Milwaukee became an Eastern team in 1972, essentially swapping divisional spots when the Washington Senators relocated to Texas. (That was the 1961 expansion Senators, not to be confused with the team of that same name that moved from Washington to Minnesota and became the Twins after the 1960 season.) The Brewers remained in the AL East until 1994, when the switch to a three-division format landed the Brew Crew in the new AL Central with the Indians, Royals, Twins, and White Sox. Three years later, Major League Baseball wanted to add one team to each league, necessitating that another team switch leagues to accommodate the new clubs. The Brewers volunteered and became the first club to switch from the AL to the NL. The Brewers took up residence in the NL Central, making it the only six-team division in baseball.

Before interleague play, the only way fans could see a 1980 matchup between Jerry Koosman's Twins against Steve Carlton's Phillies was at a spring training game.

The Western League was a minor league in the Midwest that had failed four times before it was reorganized for the 1894 season with Ban Johnson as president. Charlie Comiskey, a standout player and manager in three different major leagues, moved into ownership in the Western League the following year. While the National League was contracting in 1899, the Western League shifted Comiskey's St. Paul franchise to Chicago. The circuit also changed its name to the American League. The AL was still under the National Agreement and could not even advertise the name Chicago—Comiskey instead grabbed the White Stockings name that Cap Anson had made famous in the NL. After the 1900 season the AL dropped out of the agreement and declared itself an equal.

Contract jumping, bidding wars, and court battles ensued as the upstart AL not only spread into abandoned NL cities, but it also went into direct competition in the NL strongholds of Boston and Philadelphia, and succeeded in outdrawing the senior circuit in Chicago and Boston. The war was on.

Why is there a National League and an American League? | **59**

Doubleheader

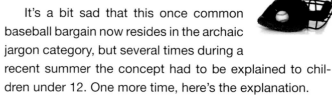

It's a bit sad that this once common baseball bargain now resides in the archaic jargon category, but several times during a recent summer the concept had to be explained to children under 12. One more time, here's the explanation.

Kids, a doubleheader—or twinbill, if you will—is two games in one day played consecutively with only 20–45 minutes between games. A regular price ticket covered admission for both games and it was once common to see twinbills on Sundays as well as Memorial Day, the Fourth of July, and Labor Day. This is what Ernie Banks was talking about when he said, "Let's play two" during his prime half a century ago. Mr. Cub wasn't saying, "Let's play a game, wait four hours, clear the stadium, the parking lot, the private clubs, and charge everybody all over for the night game." That would be a day-night doubleheader. It's a shame kids are no longer familiar with what now is often called a "straight" doubleheader because not long ago they were the main beneficiaries of the double dip for the price of one.

Boston's Cy Young dominated the pitching in the new league. William "Dummy" Hoy, given new life in the AL at age 39, was an on-base machine for AL champion Chicago, managed by pitcher Clark Griffith, who'd jumped ship from Chicago's NL club. Likewise, third baseman Jimmy Collins went from NL to AL in Boston and managed the new club to the best home record in either league while doubling his old club's 1901 attendance. Napoleon Lajoie, however, was the biggest prize. He jumped from the Philadelphia

Phillies to the Philadelphia Athletics and was the dominant hitter in the fledgling league. He not only won the Triple Crown, but his .426 average remains the highest ever recorded in the AL.

Though decidedly top heavy that first year, continued raids on the NL put the leagues more on par in 1902. The Milwaukee Brewers shifted to St. Louis and the relocated and renamed Browns nearly caught the AL champion Athletics, but Philadelphia had its own problems. A court dispute over Lajoie forced the A's to send the star second baseman to Cleveland. John McGraw, meanwhile, feuded with AL president Ban Johnson and tried to bring down the Baltimore franchise. When Johnson suspended McGraw, he jumped to the New York Giants and scattered the best Orioles to the NL, showing which side he was on in the league war. Ban Johnson lodged a thorn in McGraw's side in 1903 by moving the Orioles to New York, where they eventually became known as the Yankees.

The leagues agreed to a peace treaty in 1903, though feuds would linger for years—the Giants' refusal to play the 1904 World Series being the most visible scar. The World Series would be the jewel

Vernon Wells of the Toronto Blue Jays takes a swing during an interleague game against the Colorado Rockies.

PHOTO CREDIT: SHUTTERSTOCK IMAGES

created by this forced marriage and full-blown baseball fever would spread from two-team cities to the rest of the country before the end of the decade. Just as the American Football League and National Football League would need the fierce competition of a head-to-head battle to turn their sport into a power some six decades later, it was the cross-league championship that transformed baseball into the national pastime.

Yogi's Observation

"You can observe a lot by watching."—Yogi Berra, Hall of Fame catcher

WHAT IS A MET?

Met is short for Metropolitan. It was the name of New York's American Association team in the 1880s. The second major league, the AA also provided the second major league team at the original incarnation of the Polo Grounds. While a lot of teams in this era did not have nicknames, the AA club went by Metropolitans to differentiate itself from the National League club that played on an adjoining diamond. The 1884 Mets were the first New York team to win a championship or play in a "World Series" (the nineteenth century forerunner to the league versus league championship we know today). Yet by 1888 the AA Mets were no more.

When the Giants and the Brooklyn Dodgers both left for California after the 1957 season, New York desperately wanted another National League team. New York was awarded an expansion team for the 1962 season. Owner Joan Payson favored the name Meadowlarks for her new club, but she went with Mets after a poll showed that was the name the public preferred. It wasn't such a stretch since the team's official name was already the New York Metropolitan Baseball Club, Inc. "Mets" fit on a uniform—and in a newspaper headline—much better than the team's official handle.

Fitting into headlines was a concern back when that was how most fans got their game results. That also had something to do with several other names still in use today. Let's go around the horn.

Angels—The name dates back to the founding of the Pacific Coast League in 1903. The "City of Angels" joined the American League as an expansion club in 1961. The nickname has remained, though the location has been billed as Los Angeles, California, Anaheim, and Los Angeles of Anaheim despite maintaining the same address since 1966.

Astros—Houston joined the National League the same year as the Mets in 1962. The club went by the name Colt .45s until 1964, their final year at outdoor Colt Stadium. With the team moving into its state-of-the-art domed stadium in the midst of the space race, it seemed logical that the club ditch the firearms surname and go with Astros since Houston was the command center for the space program.

Athletics—The name dates back to the amateur era of the 1860s and the Athletic Baseball Club of Philadelphia. The team turned professional in 1871 and was a founding member of the National League in 1876 before being expelled for skipping the final western trip of that year. An American Association team in Philadelphia carried the name in the 1880s. Resurrected when Philadelphia became a charter member of the American League in 1901, the name Athletics—plus a stylized "A" that dates back to the original amateur club—has remained in place (with some design updating) despite franchise moves from Philly to Kansas City to Oakland. Don't be so formal, call 'em the A's.

A colorful collage of clubs.

Somehow, Quaker or Blue Jay Phanatic just doesn't have the same ring as Phillie.

PHOTO CREDIT: SHUTTERSTOCK IMAGES

Blue Jays—Maple Leafs had been Toronto's minor league team's name, but that name was so identified with the city's hockey franchise that a panel of judges went in a different direction. The Blue Jays flew into action in 1977.

Braves—The only team to have existed every year since the first professional league in 1871, they came into being as the Boston Red Stockings. Yet the city's American League club grabbed the name Red Sox after the National League squad switched to white socks in 1907. They were subsequently called Doves, one of several names that didn't stick (along with Red Caps, Beaneaters, Nationals, and Rustlers). Braves came about in 1912, a reference to new owner James Gaffney's Tammany Hall connections (the political group was named after Tamanend, a Lenni-Lenape chief who fostered peace between the natives and settlers in the seventeenth century, hence the Indian headdress as Tammany's symbol). Boston's stunning 1914 pennant and World Series sweep got the club dubbed the "Miracle Braves." The name was further reinforced by the construction of massive Braves Field the following year. A change in ownership resulted in a switch to Bees in 1936, only to change back to Braves with new owners in 1941. It has stayed Braves through relocations to Milwaukee and Atlanta and opposition from Native Americans.

Brewers—Milwaukee was the Beer City even before an original American League entry called the Brewers left Milwaukee for St. Louis in 1902 and became the Browns. Brewers remained a minor league name in the city until the Seattle Pilots—a 1969 AL expansion team—relocated to Milwaukee just before the 1970 season and claimed the name. The Brewers later switched leagues, going National League in 1998.

Cardinals—Brown Stockings was the favored name for the St. Louis entrant in the inaugural National League season of 1876. While that team failed a year later, the 1882 American Association club took the name Brown Stockings, or Browns. The club won four straight pennants (1884–88) before joining the National League in 1892. St. Louis siphoned off many star players, including Cy Young, from the Cleveland Spiders in 1899—an egregious result of syndicate ownership—and switched from brown to red socks while calling themselves Perfectos. The new team color won out and the term "Cardinals" started appearing in print before the season was over. Unlike clubs in other cities where football teams took the name of the local baseball side, the football Cardinals were not named after the baseball team they shared a stadium with in St. Louis; the football club, which originated in Chicago, also took its name based on the team color.

Cubs—The Cubs name was a long time coming. The team, on the other hand, has remained a rock of the National League since it helped found the league

It's "T" for Texas, as four-time Texas All-Star Buddy Bell could well have told you, but the name Rangers was synonymous with Lone Star lawmen long before a group of Senators relocated from Washington.

PHOTO CREDIT: DAN CARUBIA

in 1876. The franchise, however, actually dates to 1871, the inaugural year of the game's first professional league: the National Association. (Chicago actually missed the 1872–73 NA seasons following the Great Chicago Fire.) Names for Chicago's NL club were plentiful: the first being the White Stockings, the most popular being the Colts, and the most memorable being the Orphans, a name adopted after longtime star and manager Cap Anson left for New York in 1898. Manager Frank Selee's youthful 1902 team started being called Cubs, a name that newspapers used as a tag for the youthful club. The team became a powerhouse after Frank Chance replaced the ill Selee as manager in 1905. The name Cubs was well established by 1910, when Franklin P. Adams of the *New York Evening Mail* referred to the double play trio of Tinker to Evers to Chance as a "Trio of Bearcubs, fleeter than birds." Chicago's NFL club changed its name to Bears in 1922 to play off the Cubs name.

The Royals took their name to stately heights, with majestic fountains beyond the outfield and a crown-shaped scoreboard (since replaced by a more modern but less regal video display).

Diamondbacks—It's a rattlesnake found in Arizona. Beware of both Diamondbacks and owners dumping ballplayers for prospects.

Dodgers—The club began in the American Association in 1884 as the Atlantics, a tip of the cap to the respected 1860s amateur Brooklyn club of that name. The AA club became known as the Bridegrooms when six players were married during the 1888 season. The innovation of the trolley suddenly made their supporters "Trolley Dodgers." Dodgers remained the de facto name, but the club went by Robins and Superbas due to Hall of Fame managers Wilbert Robinson and Ned Hanlon (a vaudeville troupe was known as Hanlon's Superbas and the name was affixed to the ballclub). The tag "Bums" was hung on Brooklyn by cartoonist Willard Mullin and the borough turned this perceived slight into an identity. The Dodgers left the bums, grooms, and trolleys behind for Los Angeles after the 1957 season.

Giants—The National League club picked up the name Gothams (Gotham being another name for the city) to differentiate itself from the American Association Mets in the 1880s. A boast from manager Jim Mutrie about "my giants" may be apocryphal, but the name has stuck since 1885. Despite long ago moving to California with the Dodgers, there are still Giants on both coasts—the New York football team, which spent 30 years at the Polo Grounds, took the baseball club's name in 1925.

Indians—The American League came into existence shortly after the Cleveland Spiders were eliminated by the National League following the 1899 season. Cleveland's AL club was originally the Blues and became the Naps following the arrival of superstar Nap Lajoie in 1902. When Lajoie left in 1915, ownership chose the name Indians because it played off the world champion Braves, who'd become an overnight sensation. (The story of Cleveland Spider Louis Sockalexis, a Penobscot Indian, being the inspiration for the nickname is a mostly after-the-fact tale.) Indians has remained the name even as Native American groups have protested the depiction in recent decades.

Marlins—The name reflects the successful minor league Miami Marlins, who date back to the 1950s. A marlin can weigh more than 1,000 pounds and is quite a catch.

Mariners—Mariners, like Pilots before it, referred to Seattle's nautical history. The 1969 Pilots moved to Milwaukee after one year; Seattle's expansion M's endured seemingly endless travails from their birth in 1977 until the mid-1990s. Their early fate seemed to echo the famous Samuel Taylor Coleridge poem, "The Rime of the Ancient Mariner," in which a seafaring narrator is cursed with bad luck and an albatross around his neck.

Nationals—This was among the names used by several nineteenth century major league Washington incarnations, none of which survived. The Senators were founding members of the American League in 1901, and were often referred to as the Nationals. The original Senators moved to Minnesota after the 1960 season and their 1961 expansion replacement, also called the Senators, skedaddled to Texas after 1971. Baseball did not return to Washington until 2005, with the relocation of the Montreal Expos (named after Expo '67, an international exposition held in Montreal). The franchise took the familiar Senators "W" cap and the old Nationals moniker.

Orioles—Baltimore also looked to the past when naming its present team. The American Association, National League, and American League all had Baltimore teams called the Orioles (the state bird of Maryland). The first two clubs went under; the AL entry relocated to New York in 1903 and is now known as the Yankees. When the St. Louis Browns moved to Baltimore in 1954, there was little suspense about the name, especially since a successful minor league team had operated as the Orioles during the half century the American League went missing in Maryland.

Padres—Like the Angels, the Padres originated in the Pacific Coast League. The Padres joined the PCL in 1936, taking their name for the missionaries of the region in Spanish colonial times ("padre" is Spanish for "father"). San Diego joined the National League in 1969.

Phillies—Back in the nineteenth century teams were often called by the name of their city. It's been Phillies since 1883, though the team also went by Quakers in its early years. Owner Bob Carpenter tried calling the team Blue Jays after fans chose the name in a 1940s contest, but it never caught on.

Pirates—This name came from the ballclub's actions. Born in 1882 as an American Association club hailing from Allegheny, located across the river of that name, the team jumped into the National League in 1887. The club earned its nickname by signing second baseman Louis Bierbauer in the wake of the failed Players' League in 1890. His former team, Philadelphia of the American Association, claimed Bierbauer to be their property. Though a commission upheld the signing, the team was forever branded the Pirates, a name the club embraced and took as its official name in 1891. It also provided the name for Pittsburgh's football team, which was known as the Pirates from their 1933 founding until the name changed to Steelers in 1940.

Rangers—The expansion Washington Senators moved to Texas in 1972. They were rechristened after the Texas Rangers Division, formed in 1823 and the country's oldest state-level law enforcement agency.

Rays—A devil ray (also called devil fish) is a large aquatic creature. This was news to many people who thought Devil Ray sacrilegious, offensive, or at the very least, confusing. "Devil" was officially dropped in 2008 as the team went with a sun ray theme. The perennial doormat club suddenly won the AL pennant. That's one devil of a coincidence.

Red Sox—Boston's National League club had originally been known as the Red Stockings until they abandoned red socks for white in 1907 (presumably due to fear of blood poisoning from colored socks if a player was spiked). The American League club, called Pilgrims, Puritans, Plymouth Rocks, and Somersets (among other names that didn't last), snagged the familiar label, rebranded it "Red Sox," and slapped a red sock on the uniform. And that took care of that.

Reds—The original Red Stockings date back to 1867. Two years later they were baseball's first all-professional team. Cincinnati's entry in the inaugural National League season of 1876 also went by this name, but they were bounced for selling liquor on Sundays in 1880. Reborn in the American Association, the new team became the Reds. They joined the NL in 1890 and have continued with the name except for a strategic switch to Redlegs (1953–58) during the communist scare.

Rockies—It seemed strange that Colorado's long hoped for National League expansion team did not adopt the name Denver Bears after the successful minor league club of that name. Instead they took the same name as the hockey team that lasted seven seasons before becoming the New Jersey Devils in 1982. But who can argue with naming yourself after the Rocky Mountains?

Royals—After 13 unlucky seasons by the Kansas City Athletics, the city only went without major league baseball for one year following Charlie Finley's 1968 move to Oakland. Kansas City got its own expansion club and named it after American Royal, a livestock and horse show held annually in Kansas City since 1899. Some sources claim the name Royals was also a tip of the cap to the Negro League Kansas City Monarchs. Whether it was an inspiration or not, the Royals did spend their first four seasons in Municipal Stadium, longtime home of the Monarchs.

Did You Know?

Texas Joins the Club

The Texas Rangers became the last of the 30 major league franchises to win a postseason series when they defeated the Tampa Bay Rays in the 2010 American League Division Series. The Rangers also became the first team to win every game in a postseason series on the road (Texas lost both home games in the best-of-five ALDS). The victory had been a long time coming for Texas, which came into existence as the new Washington Senators in 1961, joining the Angels as the first expansion teams of the twentieth century. Washington relocated to Texas in 1972. Rangers president Nolan Ryan, the first member of the Hall of Fame with a "T" for Texas insignia on his plaque, last enjoyed a postseason victory in 1969 at age 22, when his win clinched the first postseason series for the New York Mets. "I thought about the history of this organization and how important a step this was because we've never done it," Ryan said of the Rangers moments after the 2010 ALDS ended, "but I was also just a nervous wreck." Ryan's club went on to beat the Yankees for the 2010 pennant.

Tigers—Wolverines was the name of the successful National League franchise in Detroit in the 1880s. "Tigers" was a nickname for the city's light guard military unit whose proud history dated to the Civil War. According to author Richard Bak, the Western League ballclub received permission from the unit to use the name when the league became the American League at the turn of the century. The Tigers remain the only AL team in the same city dating back to the Western League.

Twins—The Washington Senators, an original American League club, moved to the Twin Cities of Minneapolis and St. Paul after the 1960 season. Though they actually settled in Bloomington, the team took the obvious Twins name and still use "TC" as an abbreviation for the two Minnesota cities bisected by the Mississippi River.

White Sox—The second Chicago team to enter the world with the name White Stockings, this name was permanently entrenched by the time the American League was founded in 1901. The name was shortened to White Sox in the papers and future journalists and enthusiasts would call them the Chi-Sox, Pale Hose, and South Siders, among other things.

Yankees—Relocated from Baltimore in 1903, these flown-the-coop Orioles began their New York existence at Hilltop Park, located on the highest point in Manhattan. The name Highlanders sounded right, but the name needed altering when the team moved to the lower-lying Polo Grounds in 1913. The papers had long referred to the team as "Yankees" ("Yanks" for short) and the moniker—another name for an American or Northerner—became universal. Even the Giants, whose fans had called the AL club the Invaders when they arrived from Baltimore, called the Yankees tenants for a decade. Dominating baseball on and off since their move to Yankee Stadium in 1923, they've been called everything from the Bronx Bombers to the Evil Empire.

Fungo

To fungo is to pick up a ball, toss it in the air, and hit it. Before games, coaches can be seen hitting fungoes to players during batting practice, though the glory days of fungoes are in the past. In the early years of the twentieth century, Cy Young was said to be such an expert at hitting fungoes that Tris Speaker, one of the great center fielders of all time, credited the legendary pitcher's ability to hit balls just out of reach with teaching Speaker to better anticipate where a ball would go even before it was hit. A fungo bat is often longer and lighter than normal bats, which can help the fungo hitter place the ball to a precise spot. Though newer parks have often done away with them, most ballparks used to have fungo circles, located not far from home plate. Those safe havens for fungo hitters should not be confused with the on-deck circles, which are located closer to the dugout.

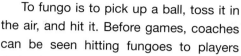

A Gummy Business

"Baseball is too much of a sport to be called a business, and too much of a business to be called a sport."—Philip Wrigley, Cubs and confectionary executive

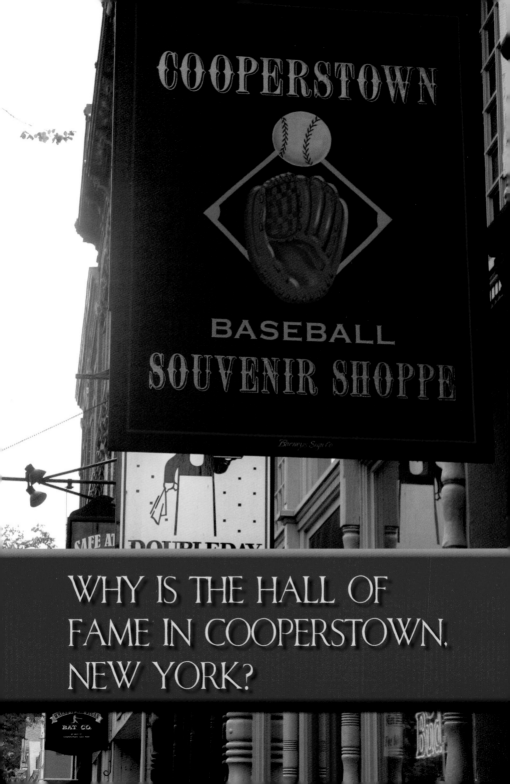

COOPERSTOWN

BASEBALL
SOUVENIR SHOPPE

WHY IS THE HALL OF
FAME IN COOPERSTOWN,
NEW YORK?

It seems just like baseball to put the Hall of Fame in the same state as one of the most visited cities in the world, yet locate the institution far enough away from the city to make it as difficult as possible for tourists to visit. But at the same time, the National Baseball Hall of Fame is not just another museum to click off on a tourist's Manhattan itinerary. It is a pilgrimage where those who clearly seek it out will be enriched by the journey. It helps if you like baseball.

So why Cooperstown, New York? To use the sports vernacular: Cooperstown wanted it. No, Cooperstown needed it. A small resort town on Otsego Lake with long winters, short summers, and beautifully crisp autumns, Cooperstown was in trouble as the Depression deepened in the 1930s. Prohibition had made things even worse, stripping the value from its hops fields; a subsequent blight on the crop only made matters worse. Cooperstown had made its name based on two patents. Its benefactor, the Clark Family, held half the patent on the Singer sewing machine and forged its wealth in the nineteenth century on the business side of this time-saving necessity. The town took its name from the novelist James Fenimore Cooper's father,

The National Baseball Hall of Fame and Museum in Cooperstown, New York.

Judge William Cooper, who obtained letters patent to large tracks of land in the area and moved there with his family and infant son in 1790. The area was forever called the Leatherstocking region for Cooper's fabled series of novels known as "Leatherstocking Tales," which included *The Last of the Mohicans* and *The Deerslayer*.

The town had history—and literature—but what Cooperstown needed was something that would really bring in the people. A Clark Foundation employee, Alexander Cleland, was stretching his legs after a meeting when he came across a ballfield being attended to by laborers from the Works Progress Administration. As Bill James reported in *Whatever Happened to the Hall of Fame*:

Cleland saw work in progress on a WPA project to improve Doubleday Field, which is where baseball could have been invented, if only those other people hadn't invented it first.

Cleland hit on the idea for a baseball museum in good old Cooperstown. His concept collided with another idea bandied about for a baseball Hall of Fame. There had been attempts at creating a baseball monument listing the game's greats in Washington, D.C., but Congress never stepped to the plate with the funding. Cleland's idea had the approval of the Clarks and organized baseball.

By 1936 Cooperstown had its first class of ballplayers in the first sports Hall of Fame in the United States, even though the museum had yet to be built. The first class set the standard for those who would follow: Ty Cobb, Walter Johnson, Christy Mathewson, Babe Ruth, and Honus Wagner. The museum, built at a cost of $100,000, opened in 1939 and the crowds have been coming ever since.

The Hall of Fame has indeed been great for the game and town. Despite the Farmers Museum, Fenimore Museum, Glimmerglass Opera House, Brewery Ommegang, and other attractions located in the little burg, the name Cooperstown has become synonymous with the Hall of Fame. When someone is "elected to Cooperstown" it is immediately known without further explanation needed that the person has been chosen to stand among a select few so honored in the game's long history. All this in a town with barely 2,000 full-time residents as of 2010. Cooperstown is not easy to find, yet the idea that Alexander Cleland wrote on his original proposal could draw "hundreds of visitors per year," brings in some 300,000 people to Cooperstown annually. As for the town's legitimacy as the place where baseball was invented, that's a different matter entirely.

In 1905 a commission was put together to decide once and for all whether the game of baseball derived from the British game of rounders or was a purely American invention. The commission was put together by sporting good manufacture and former pitcher Albert Spalding, who certainly had a dog in this fight. Former National League president A. G. Mills led the commission, which included Spalding and four distinguished persons of the day.

The Mills Commission accepted the correspondence of a mining engineer Abner Graves, who had known Abner Doubleday as a boy in the 1830s; Graves later wound up in a home for the criminally insane after killing his wife. The commission embraced the flimsy evidence of Doubleday's role in baseball's founding while ignoring the stacks of evidence that claimed otherwise. Yet let the record show, it was not a rubber stamp finding as has long been assumed.

Author John Thorn came across the Mills Commission's papers, which had previously been thought destroyed in a 1913 fire. In a 2007 article in the journal *Nine*, Thorn reported:

Mills and his factotum, James A. Sullivan, had in fact done rather a lot of work. Spreading their net wide, they had drawn forth amazingly clearheaded reminiscences by octogenarian ballplayers and scribes, and Sullivan's raw, unedited files offer many treasures not present in the summaries that scholars have previously accessed. Indeed, Mills and Sullivan, not at all the lackeys they had been made out to be, digested the Doubleday concoction

with so much distaste that they continued their search for better evidence even after the commission's mandate ended on December 31, 1907.

Mills, who had known Abner Doubleday, had never heard the man mention baseball. Yet at the end of the day, his commission went with the Doubleday story, which meant siding with Spalding and the sporting goods empire and the America-first crowd. According to the "official" story on the invention of the game put forth in the first Hall of Fame program in 1939, the special commission "declared unqualifiedly that the proof was sufficient and pronounced the game American to the core."

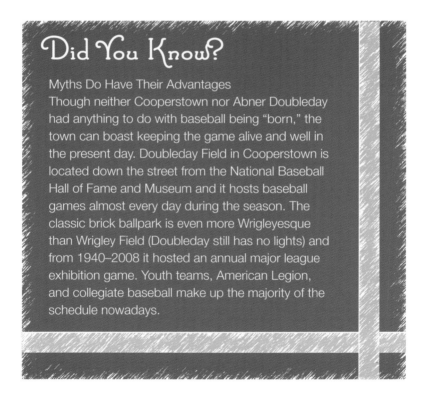

Did You Know?

Myths Do Have Their Advantages
Though neither Cooperstown nor Abner Doubleday had anything to do with baseball being "born," the town can boast keeping the game alive and well in the present day. Doubleday Field in Cooperstown is located down the street from the National Baseball Hall of Fame and Museum and it hosts baseball games almost every day during the season. The classic brick ballpark is even more Wrigleyesque than Wrigley Field (Doubleday still has no lights) and from 1940–2008 it hosted an annual major league exhibition game. Youth teams, American Legion, and collegiate baseball make up the majority of the schedule nowadays.

OFFICIAL PROGRAM
Doubleday•Field
"The Birthplace of Baseball"
Cooperstown   New York
1839   1939
baseball
Centennial

Copyright Baseball Centennial, Inc.

The program for the opening of the Hall of Fame in Cooperstown in 1939.

Abner Doubleday was a good leader—if you were going into battle. A veteran of the Mexican War, he fired the first shot in defense of Fort Sumter at the start of the Civil War, rose to the rank of major general in the Union Army, and fought effectively in some of the conflict's bloodiest fighting at Antietam and Gettysburg, suffering a neck wound in the latter action. His military record has become secondary in history to his invented part in the invention of baseball, a game he never claimed to have any interest in during his 73 years of life. He had a lot more to do with the development of the cable car, which he held patent on during his command in San Francisco in the 1870s. And Doubleday, whose family had already moved from Cooperstown earlier in the 1830s, was downstate at West Point as a 20-year-old cadet at the time he was supposedly in Elihu Phinney's cow pasture in 1839. It was there, according to the original Hall of Fame program, that he "traced the pattern of a baseball field on a diamond . . . laid down a set of rules for a group of boys and called it baseball." He might as well have called it macaroni, as far as the truth goes.

Cooperstown's Doubleday Field: Not where the game was invented, but a place where the game is kept alive quite nicely.

Golden Sombrero

The golden sombrero is achieved by striking out four times in one game. Since a hat trick signifies three, a larger hat is needed for four. A rare feat in past generations, more players swinging for the fences have littered dugouts with the mythical headgear. On the ball announcers will declare a player striking out five times in a game to have earned a platinum sombrero; six whiffs, only achieved eight times in extra-inning games, is called a titanium sombrero. *Ay yi yi.*

QUOTABLE

Shoeless and Cute

"My own opinion is that the people who want to put Joe Jackson into the Hall of Fame are baseball's answer to those women who show up at murder trials wanting to marry the cute murderer." — Bill James, writer

The little k Play.

BASE-BALL.

THE *Ball* once ſtruck off,
   Away flies the *Boy*
To the next deſtin'd Poſt,
   And then Home with Joy.

MORAL.
Thus *Britons* for Lucre
   Fly over the Main ;
But, with Pleaſure tranſported,
   Return back again.

TRAP-

SO WHO INVENTED BASEBALL?

Nobody. Which means everybody.

"Historians saw little need to study the origins of the game because the question appeared to have been resolved," wrote David Block in *Baseball Before We Knew It*. Like many people who grew up obsessed with baseball in the Baby Boom years after World War II, the concept that Cooperstown was the birthplace of baseball with Abner Doubleday its creator was, as Block recalled, "an unassailable truth." This adopted piece of historical fancy stunted searches into the game's origins for decades.

While it now seems foolish that very few questioned that a future general simply invented the game one day and then headed back

Did You Know?

Starting on Monday
The first player taken in the first amateur player draft in 1965 was Rick Monday, selected by the Kansas City A's. One of eight players drafted that year out of Arizona State University, Monday went on to a 19-year career as an outfielder with the A's (in Kansas City and Oakland), the Chicago Cubs, and Los Angeles Dodgers. He hit 241 career home runs, plus a ninth-inning homer that decided the 1981 National League pennant, but Monday is best remembered for rescuing an American flag from burning at Dodger Stadium in 1976. Of the 824 players selected in the original draft, 82 went on to play major league ball, including Monday's ASU and A's teammate Sal Bando, Bernie Carbo, Ray Fosse, Ken Holtzman (traded for Monday in 1971), Graig Nettles, Amos Otis, Freddie Patek, and future Hall of Famers Johnny Bench and Nolan Ryan.

Gopher Ball

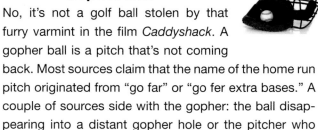

No, it's not a golf ball stolen by that furry varmint in the film *Caddyshack*. A gopher ball is a pitch that's not coming back. Most sources claim that the name of the home run pitch originated from "go far" or "go fer extra bases." A couple of sources side with the gopher: the ball disappearing into a distant gopher hole or the pitcher who served it up wanting to crawl into a hole and hide.

to West Point, there was a precedent for the one-man, one-game invention theory of popular sports. Basketball was pretty much invented by a YMCA instructor in 1891. James A. Naismith even created it on demand, as his boss at the Springfield Y gave him two weeks to come up with something students could play indoors during the coming Massachusetts winter. Softball had likewise been devised inside a Chicago gymnasium one afternoon in 1887 by George Hancock.

In truth, by the end of the nineteenth century people had been playing baseball for decades and its precursor had been played for centuries. Block notes references to the game we now know as baseball in England in the eighteenth century. A woodcut from 1744 shows three men and three bases—stakes, to be precise—with one offering the ball as if to pitch. There is no bat since this early version could also be played by hitting the ball with one's hand. How do we know this is baseball? The illustration from *A Little Pretty Pocket-Book* is called "Base-Ball."

Whether you spell it as one word or two, playing the game without this is baseless.

PHOTO CREDIT: SHUTTERSTOCK IMAGES

Living in the Red

"Ninety feet between home plate and first base may be the closest man has ever come to perfection."
—Red Smith, journalist

The *Ball* once struck off
Away flies the *Boy*
To the next destin'd Port,
And then Home with Joy.

Block goes back, way back, to thirteenth century illustrations from Spain and Flanders that depict something that looks an awful lot the game we are so familiar with today. The rules changed but the ball and the bat—or at least someone's hand imitating the bat—seem familiar, regardless of what people called these games. But just as it is hard to feel connected to ancestors one imagines walking the streets of medieval Europe, keep in mind that the case can be made for bat and ball games in Egypt dating back to fifteen centuries *before Christ*.

Back on American shores, the fellows in Cooperstown even noted when the Hall of Fame opened in 1939, "Ballplaying itself probably could be traced to the Garden of Eden. They tell of monkeys swinging at coconuts with the branches of trees." Author John Thorn, who probably knows as much about the game's origins as anyone, titled his 2011 book on the birth of the game *Baseball in the Garden of Eden*.

"Well, baseball in its roundball (Massachusetts or New England) form goes as far back as 1735," Thorn said when queried about the discoveries in his new work. "But the New York Game, the one that endured, certainly dates to the 1830s and perhaps as early as the 1780s."

Obviously, what we know as baseball developed from other games, be it townball, roundball, rounders, and one old cat all the way to four old cat. All of it derived from earlier incarnations that came from the Old World. The New World made base-ball into base ball and the twentieth century made it baseball. And it was good.

There have been champions of the single inventor idea, including those who claim Manhattan bookseller and volunteer fireman Alexander Cartwight as "Father of Baseball." Alexander established the Knickerbocker ballclub and a set of rules in 1845, but bat and ball games were well known even before Cartwright's twenty rules were written down. Alexander, who left New York in 1849 and wound up in Honolulu, is unquestionably father of the game in Hawaii.

Members of the group charged with uncovering the unequivocal origin of the game, the Mills Commission, notably Albert Spalding, had an agenda to see that the game arose on these shores. British-born sportswriter Henry Chadwick, also dubbed with that familiar sobriquet, "Father of Baseball," insisted even after the Mills Commission released its findings in 1907 that baseball developed from English rounders. Spalding was adamant that America's game was made in America, despite arguments from many sources that contacted the commission, notably Henry Sargent. To quote one letter:

I have stated this to you before. I repeat it now, because I find that everyone who remembers round ball at all, agrees with me. So if round ball is the English rounders, and the difference between Mr. Chadwick and Mr. Spaulding (sic) is whether baseball sprung from rounders or from four old cat, there is no difference between them. They are talking about the same thing, only they do not know it.

Go down the road, across the pond, around the world, or back in time . . . the answer is the same: Baseball had many fathers. Those who played the game loved it enough to keep developing baseball and passing it along. The game proved as adaptable as the people who played it.

WHY IS THE SPITBALL
ILLEGAL?

The history of the spitball tells more about baseball's attitude toward cheating than it does about a pitch that's difficult to hit. The spitball began in baseball as a legal pitch. It was outlawed in 1920, but its top practitioners were allowed to continue using it. And in recent decades the pitch has been accepted with a wink even as hitters using performance-enhancing substances have been subjected to far more scrutiny by the game and society.

A spitball is thrown by putting a foreign substance on the ball, whether it is spit, sweat, emery board, Vaseline, or a similar substance. (We'll include the modern version of the scuffball and pine tar pitch in this category since that defaces the ball as well.) Generally thrown with a fastball motion, the altered spot on one side of the ball creates unpredictable movement, often at the last instant. It generally moves like a knuckleball, only it's thrown harder—and illegally.

Though legendary sportswriter Hugh Fullerton claimed that pitcher Tom Bond threw the first spitball using glycerin in New Bedford, Massachusetts, in 1876, and others may have dabbled with the "aqueous pitch," the pitch did not come into prominence for another quarter century. Elmer Stricklett was hailed as the inventor of the twentieth century spitter, but a 1913 article in *Baseball Magazine* by former minor leaguer P. A. Meaney credited Frank Corridon with developing the spitball. Meaney explained that while warming up before a minor league game in Providence in 1902, the 21-year-old Corridon "absentmindedly wet his fingers and applied them to the ball, which he cut loose with all the speed he had. The result astonished him, the ball taking the sharpest kind of break from its original course." Corridon, thrilled by this new pitch, called over outfielder George Hildebrand and asked him to grab a bat—both were astonished at the ball's movement. Hildebrand moved on to Sacramento, where he showed Stricklett the pitch and the cult of the spitballer grew exponentially.

Jack Chesbro, whose team was victimized by Stricklett's spitter in California in the fall of 1902, soon mastered both the pitch and the American League. He won an astonishing 41 games in 1904 thanks to his miracle pitch. Yet it was a spitball that flew over the head of catcher Jack "Red" Kleinow and cost his New York Highlanders the pennant against Boston on the last day of the 1904 season. Big Ed Walsh, the only other pitcher since 1891 to win 40 games in a season, relied on the spitter to turn the trick for the 1908 White Sox. When Meaney wrote the spitball article in 1913, he claimed that "many of the foremost baseball men of the day regard Walsh as the premier pitcher of all time." With that kind of success, others took up the wet one, including White Sox teammate Ed Cicotte—though Cicotte picked up his shine ball, not from Walsh but from another future Hall of Famer, Red Faber. Former legal spitball practitioner Frank Shellenback described the Cicotte process in a 1948 piece in *Baseball Digest*:

Eddie darkened the ball on one side by rubbing it in the dirt. Then he slickened the ball by rubbing it vigorously on his pants. The process camouflaged the ball perfectly. The ball, thrown with blazing speed, rotating quickly, and showing the white side only at split-second intervals, baffled batters completely.

With a shine ball thrown from varying deliveries as part of an arsenal that included a superb knuckleball and an unhittable pitch known as "the sailor," Cicotte emerged as one of the top pitchers in the American League. Unfortunately, White Sox owner Charlie Comiskey didn't reward him accordingly and Cicotte sought his payday elsewhere. As Chicago's top starter he was probably as responsible as any player for throwing the 1919 World Series. A year later Cicotte was out of the game because of his part in the scandal, following his indictment with the seven other Black Sox.

In a country where prohibition was the new law of the land, and a flu pandemic had killed more people worldwide than the recently concluded Great War, many questioned the ethical aspects of the spitball. Though defacing a baseball could result in a $5 fine, the

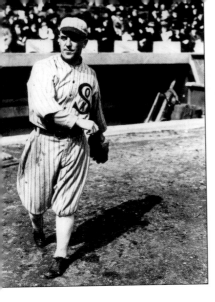

Eddie Cicotte threw the shine ball and the World Series. Note the dirty right pants leg where he shined up his signature pitch.
PHOTO CREDIT: NATIONAL BASEBALL HALL OF FAME LIBRARY, COOPERSTOWN, NY

rule was never enforced on the field. It was pretty clear that allowing pitchers to do whatever they wanted to the baseball did nothing for offense—and owners who had sweated through the financial and manpower strains of World War I felt that more hitting would attract more people to the park. So in 1920 the spitball was banned, though each team was allowed to designate up to two pitchers to throw the pitch through the season. Brooklyn's Burleigh Grimes and Cleveland's Stan Coveleski threw the pitch with impunity in the World Series: Grimes blanked the Indians in Game 2 and Coveleski allowed just two runs over three complete-game wins for the victorious Tribe.

The major leagues relented on the ban of existing spitballers in December 1920, decreeing that seventeen practitioners of the spitball could continue without penalty for the rest of their careers. Several minor league pitchers were similarly grandfathered, but they could not bring the pitch with them to big leagues. The aforementioned Frank Shellenback was essentially trapped in the Pacific Coast League with his spitball. He won a PCL-record 295 games (315 minor league wins overall), but he never pitched in the majors after 1919.

Since the 1934 retirement of Burleigh Grimes, no pitcher has thrown a legal spitball in the big leagues, but plenty have gotten away with it. The spitball went underground and few ever publicly admitted throwing it. As was the case even when it was legal, some pitchers got more mileage from batters thinking they were throwing a spitball than they did from the hard-to-control pitch. The exception, however, was Gaylord Perry.

While there is much talk about performance enhancing drugs and whether players suspected of using them should be allowed into the Hall of Fame, Perry is the first player in history to cheat his way into Cooperstown. Before the spitball, there were questions whether Perry would make it as a big league starter. At age 25, he still had yet to break into San Francisco's rotation, but his career forever changed after he was summoned in the thirteenth inning of the second game of a doubleheader at brand-new Shea Stadium on May 31, 1964. Perry, who'd picked up the spitter from teammate Bob Shaw, used the pitch consistently for the first time that night, tossing 10 shutout innings against the Mets in a 23-inning game that at the time was the longest completed game in major league history. And Perry won it. He subsequently won a permanent job in the rotation, a Cy Young Award in each league, and a spot in Cooperstown. The 314-game winner had an elaborate pre-pitch routine where he touched various places on his body in rapid succession, like a street hustler in a shell game. Finding where an illegal substance was hidden on his person was as difficult for umpires as hitting a solid ball off Perry was for hitters.

He dared anyone to catch him in the act, writing a mid-career book called *Me & the Spitter*. Others were more protective of his secret. A TV reporter sitting with the Perry family during a 1971 playoff game asked five-year-old Allison Perry if her father threw a spitball. She replied, "It's a hard slider."

Many pitchers threw a "hard slider," or something like it. During the 1960s and early 1970s the number of spitballers was arguably as high as at any time since the 1910s. Offense predictably reached Dead Ball Era levels. A 1968 anti-spitball rule was enacted to prohibit a pitcher going to his mouth. The penalty was to call a ball if no one was on base and a balk if runners were aboard. (Pitchers could go to their mouths if it was deemed cold enough that blowing on the pitching hand was a necessity to stay warm.) A rule was stiffened in 1974 so an umpire could declare an illegal pitch without evidence: a warning would be issued to a pitcher suspected of throwing a

Did You Know?

Your Grandfather's Spitball
At a March 2010 press conference in Scottsdale, Arizona, Gaylord Perry asked commissioner Bud Selig to repeal an unspecified rule, presumably rule 8.02, which forbids putting an illegal substance on the ball. Not that Perry ever paid attention to the rule during his spitballing hayday. "I want to make a comeback," the 72-year-old Hall of Famer said as the whole room chuckled. One has to wonder if one day a similar joke from a former steroid user might elicit hilarity. The spitball was once indeed a legal pitch, but even after it was wiped out in 1920, a select few were granted permission to keep using it. It was too late for Eddie Cicotte, who was banned for life for his part in the throwing the 1919 World Series, but seventeen other spitballers were given new life in 1921 as stipulated by the grandfather spitball clause:

Spitballer	Last Year
Doc Ayers	1921
Ray Caldwell	1921
Phil Douglas	1922
Dana Fillingim	1925
Marv Goodwin	1925
Dutch Leonard	1925
Allan Russell	1925
Allen Sothoron	1926
Dick Rudolph	1927
*Stan Coveleski	1928
Urban Shocker	1928

Bill Doak	1929
Clarence Mitchell	1932
*Red Faber	1933
Jack Quinn	1933
*Burleigh Grimes	1934

*Denotes Hall of Famer.
Ray Fisher was on the list but was banned from organized baseball for contract jumping before he could use the legal spitter.

spitball, followed by ejection if a second instance occurred. Perry was suspended for throwing a spitter for the only time in his career at age 43 in 1982, a few months after becoming the first pitcher in 19 years to reach 300 career wins. The umpire didn't even check the ball.

Pitches with natural sink became more prevalent, but a few pitchers still had admitted help. Defacing the ball led to suspensions for Don Sutton (1978) and Joe Niekro (1987), who compiled 545

QUOTABLE

Legally Gross

"[Bugs] Raymond, when pitching, chewed slippery elm incessantly and the spittle thus produced when applied to the ball gave it an extraordinary sharp break." —P. A. Meaney, minor leaguer

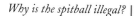

Gyro Ball

When Daisuke Matsuzaka first came to the United States in 2007, there was much talk about the gyro ball. Many claimed the pitch did not exist. Matsuzaka claimed he didn't throw one. Yale physicist Robert Adair, author of *The Physics of Baseball*, told *Popular Mechanics* the pitch indeed existed but "it's of no use in baseball." The gyro ball, as advertised, is spinning like a football along the axis where the ball is moving. This does almost nothing to [a] baseball. It's a nothing pitch." Adair did, however, claim the pitch to be effective after it bounces off the ground, known as a "googely" in cricket. Denied or derided, the pitch has an inventor, Kazushi Tezuka, a trainer who came up with it in the mid-1990s after playing with a toy gyroscope and applying the same football-like throwing motion to a baseball. Thrown with a four-seam grip the ball comes in fast; thrown with a two-seam grip comes in like a changeup. But the ball doesn't move and batters are often surprised when it doesn't. Hence, pitchers can get outs with this "nothing pitch." If it existed.

career wins between them. Hall of Famer Steve Carlton and 1986 NL Cy Young winner Mike Scott, among others, were never caught, but their alleged scuffing could drive opponents to distraction and keep them swinging at balls in the dirt all game.

A breakthrough in the search for evidence occurred during the 2006 World Series. In Game 2 in Detroit, a TV closeup of Tigers starter Kenny Rogers's pitching hand showed a discolored smudge near his thumb in the first inning. Cardinals manager Tony LaRussa asked to inspect the crafty lefty's hand as the second inning began, but Rogers had cleaned up. He cleaned the Cardinals before the night was over, allowing just two hits in eight innings in Detroit's lone win of the Series. Somewhere Frank Corridon had to be smiling . . . and wetting his fingers.

Beginning with a 23-inning game in 1964, Gaylord Perry's spitball saved San Francisco's staff for a day and helped launch a Hall of Fame career.

PHOTO CREDIT: NATIONAL BASEBALL HALL OF FAME LIBRARY, COOPERSTOWN, NY

WHY DO MANAGERS WEAR UNIFORMS IN THE DUGOUT?

L ike a lot of things in baseball, wearing a uniform is part of the game's tradition. And like a lot of traditions it has a practical explanation if you go back far enough.

Teams had men holding roles as dugout administrators in the nineteenth century, often acting as traveling secretaries or business managers. The field manager was usually the team's best—or smartest—player, and as such, the other ballplayers were likely to listen to him. He set the lineup, enforced the rules (to the level of his interest in breaking them), and in many cases had more responsibilities of the day-to-day running of the club in personnel matters than a modern manager. Wearing the uniform is a tradition that carries over from that time. It just goes with the job.

Player-managers were still somewhat popular through World War II. Cleveland's Lou Boudreau was named "Boy Manager" of the Indians at the age of 24 in 1942, becoming the youngest manager to begin a season at the post. He devised the "Ted Williams Shift," an innovation employed on even more pull hitters today than in Boudreau's time. He also realized that Bob Lemon's arm was too good to remain in center field and put him on the mound . . . and on his way to the Hall of Fame. Boudreau wound up in Cooperstown as well. He was American League MVP in 1948, the last player to earn the award while also managing a team. MVPs have also been won by player-managers Mickey Cochrane with the Detroit Tigers in 1934, and Rogers Hornsby, who did it with two different teams: the St. Louis Cardinals in 1925 and Chicago Cubs in 1929. The last player-managers in each league were Don Kessinger with the 1979 White Sox and Pete Rose with the Cincinnati Reds (1984–86).

While tradition dictates that managers wear a uniform, there are exceptions. Hall of Fame manager Joe McCarthy wore a uniform, but he never had a number on his back with the Yankees or Red Sox even though he continued managing two decades after everyone else was uniformly numbered.

And then there's Connie Mack. The most famous manager not to wear a uniform, he had ironically been a player-manager in uniform

Cornelius Alexander McGilli-cuddy, shortened to Connie Mack as a player to fit into scorecards in the nineteenth century, ruled the dugout as manager for the first half of the twentieth century, dressed for the part in a trade-mark suit and tie, and sometimes hat.

with Pittsburgh from 1894–96. When Ban Johnson decided to take the American League national—so to speak—Mack was on board from the get-go, helping talk National League players into jumping to teams all over the American League. Mack was in a suit and tie for the first Philadelphia Athletics game on April 26, 1901. For the next half century he remained in that outfit in the dugout—word has it that it wasn't the same suit all that time. Mr. Mack, as everyone called him no matter how well they knew him, directed players by pointing a rolled up scorecard and was considered one of the most low-key yet respected managers in history. And with a record of 3,731–3,948 he was winningest—and losingest—manager of all time. It helped that he also owned the team and kept himself on the job until the ripe old age of 87. So there's something to be said for wearing a tie in the dugout, which Ed Barrow, Burt Shotton, and a handful of other managers have also done.

Some managers don't like the uniform idea even today, but maybe it's better than letting skippers pick out their own outfits for the game. Or else they could essentially become unshapely models for whatever the league apparel outfitter prepares for them to wear, such as in the National Football League, where even a suit worn on the sidelines by a head coach must be tailored by Reebok. When the *Wall Street Journal*'s Tim Marchman asked Twins manager Ron Gardenhire about the subject of managing out of uniform in 2009, Gardenhire said simply, "I hate sports coats."

Hot Corner

Since hitters are predominantly right-handed, third base has long been considered the hot corner. First base certainly sees its share of hot shots, but first baseman don't have to worry about making a long throw or can run to the bag. According to *Paul Dickson's Baseball Dictionary*, the origin of the term dates to 1889 Cincinnati third baseman Hick Carpenter, who, in the words of contemporary writer Ren Mumford, "fielded seven sharp drives that almost tore him apart. The Brooklyns had old Hick at the hot corner all afternoon and it's a miracle he wasn't murdered."

Phillies manager Dallas Green comes out to remove Dick Ruthven in 1980—but there's nothing either of them can do about those baby blue uniforms.

PHOTO CREDIT: DAN CARUBIA

Did You Know?

Pitching in a Pinch
The 1905 Philadelphia Athletics had a 1.47 World Series ERA—and lost. In fact, the A's won only one game. Why? Because the New York Giants had an ERA of 0.00. Christy Mathewson threw three shutouts, Joe "Iron Man" McGinnity threw another shutout and also took the Giants' only loss, allowing three unearned runs in Game 2 as Philadelphia's Chief Bender shut out the New Yorkers. It was a World Series for the ages, with three future Hall of Famers blanking the opposition in the first of three October meetings between legendary managers John McGraw of the Giants and Connie Mack of the Athletics (whose club would beat New York in 1911 and 1913).

QUOTABLE

Words to Live By (Unless You're in a Dome)

"You don't save a pitcher for tomorrow. Tomorrow it may rain."—Leo Durocher, Hall of Fame manager

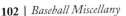

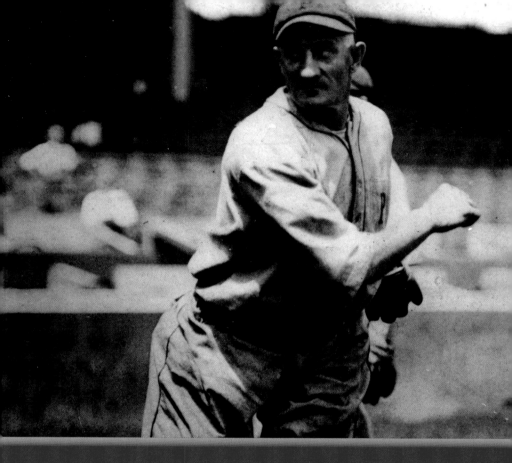

THE NAMES FOR
BASEMAN, OUTFIELDERS,
PITCHER, AND CATCHER
MAKE SENSE—BUT WHY
"SHORTSTOP"?

Shortstop is considered the most important defensive position on the baseball diamond next to catcher, but it was the last of the positions developed. In the early days of the game basemen manned their positions standing on the bases while three to six others roamed the outfield. One thing everyone noticed was that balls kept being hit between second and third. The problem seemed incurable.

Dr. Daniel Adams made the bold move to fill the gap in the infield. His original reason was not so much to field balls hit to that area but to relay throws from the outfield. He took the position for the first time in 1849 or 1850 while playing for the New York Knickerbockers. Esteemed baseball historian John Thorn notes, "The early Knickerbocker ball was so light that it could not be thrown even 200 feet, thus the need for a short fielder to send the ball in to the pitcher's point."

Doc Adams could do it all, including making the balls himself and turning the bats. Adams finally found a Scottish saddle maker who had a better method of making balls, using the horsehide "such as was used for whip lashes," the good doctor said. "I used to make the stuffing out of three or four ounces of rubber cuttings, wound with yarn and then covered with the leather." As the balls became wound tighter and could be thrown—and hit—farther, Adams and the shortstops that followed were able to play closer to the infield.

Like base ball, the position originated as two words. Paul Dickson explains in his *Baseball Dictionary* that it was "probably created to better describe the defensive function of the job performed in the short field." So contrary to what you may have heard on the schoolyard, diminutive height has never been a requirement to play shortstop, though 1970s shortstops Fred Patek (listed as 5-foot-4 on his baseball card) and Harry Chappas (measured by announcer Harry Caray as 5-foot-3) certainly lived up to the name.

A unique name is appropriate for the position on the field where teams often put their best athlete, be it Little League or major league. The position was considered so crucial for many years that teams carried these superior fielders and considered any offensive output

At 5-foot-4, shortstop Freddie Patek lived up to the position's name, but he came up big when turning the double play for the successful Royals clubs of the 1970s.

PHOTO CREDIT: NATIONAL BASEBALL HALL OF FAME LIBRARY, COOPERSTOWN, NY

Shortstop Derek Jeter acknowledges the crowd after breaking Lou Gehrig's mark of 1,269 hits at Yankee Stadium in 2008. He topped Gehrig's record for most hits as a Yankee (2,721) the following year.

PHOTO CREDIT: DAN CARUBIA

from them to be a bonus. That trend has changed in recent years with the dominance of hard-hitting big men like Cal Ripken and Derek Jeter.

Honus Wagner, an eight-time batting champion still considered to be among the greatest players in the game's history, was a rare specimen in many regards. The eight-time batting champion's offensive skills are incomparable to those of fellow Hall of Fame shortstop Ozzie

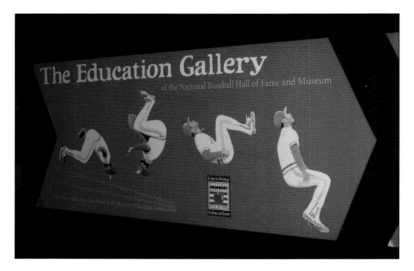

Shortstop Ozzie Smith's 13 Gold Gloves got him in the Hall of Fame, but the 15-time All-Star also collected 2,460 hits.

Smith, and you can't compare the rocky infields the Flying Dutchman faced in the early twentieth century with the artificial surfaces that the Wizard of Oz played on for most of his career. Yet both men were enshrined in Cooperstown with more than 90 percent of the vote the first time they came up for election: Wagner in the inaugural 1936 class and Smith in 2002. And that's the long and short of it.

Spoken Like a Career .256 Hitter

"When you're in a slump, it's almost as if you look out at the field and it's one big glove." — Vance Law, infielder

Did You Know?

Long-Running Program

The original New York Mets announcing crew of Ralph Kiner, Bob Murphy, and Lindsey Nelson worked together longer than any broadcast trio in baseball history. They started in 1962 and worked together through 1978, when Nelson, also a nationally known football broadcaster, left to do San Francisco Giants games. Murphy broadcast the Mets through 2003 and Kiner worked several games for the Mets in 2010. Added together, that's 108 seasons announcing Mets games. All three are honored in Cooperstown: Nelson and Murphy with the Ford C. Frick Award for broadcasting; Kiner with induction to the Hall of Fame in 1975 for his feats as a slugger in the 1940s and 1950s, which included an unprecedented seven straight home run crowns.

Montreal shortstop Tony Bernazard prepares to catch an infield pop-up.

PHOTO CREDIT: DAN CARUBIA

The names for baseman, outfielders, pitcher, and catcher make sense—but why "shortstop"? | **107**

Infield Fly Rule

An infield fly is called when a ball is popped up over the infield with less than two outs with runners on first and second or the bases loaded. The umpire generally makes the call shortly after the ball is airborne and a fielder appears to have a bead on it. The batter is declared out and runners can advance at their own risk. The reason for the call is to keep fielders from letting the ball drop and getting a double play because the runners on base have no chance to avoid a force play or double play. (It's for this reason that the infield fly is not called when there is simply a runner on first; even if the ball is dropped the batter should be running hard enough not to get doubled up.) The trouble occurs when an infield fly is not caught. Surprised runners often try to take off for the next base, even though they are not required to do so. Every season there are a few doozies that occur when an infield fly is muffed and it can live on for years as "bloopers" shown between innings on the big board at ballparks.

WHAT IS THE LOSS
COLUMN AND WHY IS
IT SO IMPORTANT?

You know the baseball races are getting tight when a broadcaster utters the phrase that a team holds a slight advantage in the "all-important loss column." If division titles, wild cards, and back in the day, pennants, are decided based on a team's number of wins, then what is so important about the loss column?

An explanation comes from the late reporter Jack Lang, who served as longtime executive secretary for the Baseball Writers' Association of America and earned the 1986 J. G. Taylor Spink Award at the Hall of Fame for his longtime coverage of the Brooklyn Dodgers and the New York Mets. "Why it is referred to as 'the all-important loss column' is simple. If you have played a game and lost it, you cannot erase that loss; but if you have not played a game, there is still an opportunity to win it," he wrote. "A loss is a loss is a loss. Only a game not yet played can become a victory."

The loss column comes up often late in the season because teams often have contested different numbers of games at a given juncture during the season. A half game in the "games back" column occurs when one team has played more games than the other. This evens out eventually because teams involved in a race for a post season spot will all play the same number of games. Even if it takes until the day after the season ends, games must be made up if they have a bearing on the outcome of a race.

The San Francisco Giants and San Diego Padres, for example, had a fight to the wire for the National League West division title in 2010. On Sunday, September 12, after the Giants beat the Padres 6–1, the two teams were tied for first place in the NL West with winning percentages that each rounded to .563, even though the Giants (81–63) had played two more games than the Padres (80–62). Though the clubs were tied, San Diego had a one-game advantage in the loss column. The Giants had September 13 off and the Padres won, putting them even in the win column, one game ahead in the loss column, and a half game in front overall. But having two extra games to make up hurt the Padres. After September 12, San Diego went 10–10 while the Giants were 11–7. San Francisco clinched the division title on the last day of the season at home against the Padres. The Giants went on to win the 2010 National League pennant and their first world championship since 1954, when they were still in New York.

The Miracle Mets of 1969 had remarkable pitching, but among the many breaks that went their way were the schedule and the weather. The last two months of the season the Mets played eight more games than the Cubs, the result of a number of early season rainouts that were made up in August and September. Chicago, ahead of New York by ten games in the standings and eight in the loss column on August 15, finished eight games behind the eventual world champion Mets. A white-hot team with a slew of games in hand can eat up a lot of ground in a hurry.

There was a time when the schedule did not fit together so neatly. In the first professional league, the National Association (formed in 1871) teams often stopped playing the schedule late in the year because of low attendance, dwindling finances, or a roadtrip that became too burdensome. The teams usually headed home or quit—one of the problems when the franchise fee was just $10. It took thirteen years after the National League's 1876 founding for a discrepancy over the number of games played to alter a pennant race.

The Giants won the 1889 National League pennant despite playing two fewer games than Boston, which finished one game back in the standings and two behind in the loss column. A bigger uproar occurred in the heated 1908 American League race, when Detroit led Cleveland by half a game at season's end. Unlike in the NL that fall, when a controversial tie between the Cubs and Giants was replayed after the two teams ended the season tied atop the standings, the Tigers were unable to make up a late-season rainout against Washington, and thus edged out the Indians by a half game though both clubs had the same number of wins. Who knows what might have happened if seventh-place Washington had started 20-year-old fire-balling phenom Walter Johnson? And if the White Sox had been able to make up their two rainouts and won both games, there would

Keystone

Keystone is another word for second base. Why? The plays at second base are often among the most key for determining a team's success in a game, and the architectural keystone is located at the crown of an arch. Two good reasons for classing up the second sack.

---

have been three teams with 90 wins. Cait Murphy, author of *Crazy '08*, uncovered a line in the *Plain Dealer* newspaper that sums up Cleveland's heavy heart in the fall of 1908: "There is no consolation in 'if.'"

The following year the AL would join the NL in requiring that games be made up if they had an impact on the pennant race. The rule still couldn't keep the Tigers from winning another title the last weekend

QUOTABLE

Know When to Hold 'em

"Baseball is like a poker game. Nobody wants to quit when he's losing; nobody wants you to quit when you're ahead."
—Jackie Robinson, Hall of Fame second baseman

of the season while playing one fewer game than the runner up. After a strike wiped out major league games for the first time in 1972, a questionable decision ruled out making up any games lost when the first week of the season was cancelled. The unplayed schedule was tragic for the Red Sox. They had seven games wiped out that first week while the Tigers had only six. Detroit played 156 games, finishing with an 86–70 mark. The Red Sox played one less game, and were 85–70 — a half game behind.

To be on the wrong end of any of these torturous races could disprove Tom Hanks's soliloquy in the film *A League of Their Own* stating "there's no crying in baseball." Of course, Detroit might offer a rebuttal about uneven schedules with the words of a Tiger named Tony: "They're great!"

Cleon Jones of the Mets tries to take out Cub Don Kessinger during one of the many contentious contests between the clubs in the first year of the National League East in 1969.

Did You Know?

Third Time's the Charm
The Braves are the only team to play a World Series in three different home cities. Making the trick even more impressive, they've won once in each city while making multiple World Series appearances. The Boston Braves won the 1914 World Series but lost in 1948. The Milwaukee Braves won the 1957 World Series but lost a rematch with the Yankees the following year. The Atlanta Braves reached the World Series in 1991, 1992, 1995, 1996, and 1999, winning the title only in '95. Other three-team cities have come close, but not matched the Braves' feat. The A's won world championships in Philadelphia and Oakland but not in Kansas City. The current Orioles have won three World Series in Baltimore, lost their only World Series as the St. Louis Browns in 1944, and played just one year as original American League franchise Milwaukee Brewers in 1901.

WHY DO SOME TEAMS
NOT HAVE PLAYER'S
NAMES ON THE BACK
OF THEIR UNIFORMS?

Some teams apparently like to keep their fans guessing by testing their loyalty or roster knowledge. Aspirin should be freely distributed at their parks when rosters expand in September.

The New York Yankees, Boston Red Sox, and San Francisco Giants played the 2010 season with only numbers on the backs of their home uniforms. The other twenty-seven teams wore names on the back. What's with the holdouts?

"Combination of tradition and the old-school admonition to 'play for the name on the *front* of the jersey, not the one on the back,'" explained Paul Lukas, founder of the noted blog Uni Watch. "Much easier to do if you don't put a name on the back to begin with."

For the first six decades of professional baseball, there were no uniform numbers at all. Random attempts were made here and there to number players. The Indians wore numbers on their sleeves in 1916, but the Tribe dropped the practice as did the other clubs that tried it briefly over the next dozen years. Players sometimes objected to the practice because they thought it made them look like prison convicts.

Cleveland came back to the idea in 1929, becoming the first team to permanently wear numbers on their home uniforms. The Yankees also donned numbers that year and were the first to wear numbers on home and away uniforms. The first major league game between two teams with numbers on their back occurred on May 13, 1929 in Cleveland. Indians 4, Yankees 3. That was the score, though in baseball's new lingo that could also mean Indian Joe Sewell and Yankee Babe Ruth.

As baseball's biggest draw, the Yankees made the numbers practice stick. They initially numbered players by their spots in the batting order—that's how Ruth got to be number 3 and Lou Gehrig 4. By 1932 every team in both leagues wore numbers at home and on the road, though the Philadelphia Athletics only did so on the road so as not to jeopardize the scorecard concession in Philly.

Before numbers, identifying players could be a puzzling to all but the hardcore regulars. People sitting in the stands with scorecards could deduce who was who based on where they were on the diamond or in the lineup. But before a game or when a reserve emerged from the dugout, a fan couldn't immediately tell which ballplayer it was without prior knowledge of the player's features or mannerisms—especially for those watching from far off bleachers. The introduction of numbers in the pre-TV age allowed fans who did not attend games regularly to figure out who was who by looking in the program. Numbers didn't hurt program sales, Mr. Mack.

In 1960 Bill Veeck Jr. made it so even people who didn't buy a program—and especially those watching on television—could identify players because it was spelled out on their backs. The White Sox, coming off their first pennant in forty years, took the field in 1960 with names above their numbers. Veeck, who nine years earlier had sent 3-foot-7-inch Eddie Gaedel to the plate for his St. Louis Browns bearing "1/8" on his back, knew how to make a show. The upstart American Football League stitched names on the backs of their uniforms that fall. (The National Football League didn't get with it for another decade.)

In baseball, as the 1960s rolled into the 1970s, players started having a little fun. Ken Harrelson had his nickname, "Hawk," on the back of his Indians uniform. Vida Blue used his first name on the back of his Oakland A's uniform, as did teammates Mudcat Grant and Catfish Hunter. Billy C. and Tony C. went for the shortened version of their Conigliaro name for their respective California clubs. Dick Allen's back read "Wampum 60"—not for his contract drive, but to honor his Pennsylvania hometown and his graduating class. Atlanta got creative to the point where commissioner Bowie Kuhn put his foot down when newly signed hurler Andy Messersmith wore "Channel" above his number 17—a rather blatant advertisement for Ted's Turner Broadcasting System. Last names have been the standard fare in the three decades since Messersmith was shot down, though Ichiro Suzuki wore his first name on his Mariners uniform starting in 2001.

Over time, every club other than the Yankees and Red Sox put names on the home uniforms. With the exception of the Giants, who

Ichiro Suzuki broke the mold in many ways, starting with putting his first name on the back of his Mariners jersey.

took the names off their home jerseys for their move to Pac Bell Park in 2000, most clubs found that people got used to the names on the back and didn't like them subsequently removed. When the 1999 Mets removed the names from the backs of the home uniforms twenty years after they had first sewed them on, players and fans complained enough so the names were back on the back for the following season. The Cubs and Dodgers dropped the names only to resume the practice—though in the case of the Cubs' 2005–06 experiment, plummeting jersey sales trumped other considerations. Perhaps that is also why the Yankees, the only team without names on their home *and* road uniforms, sell most of their T-shirts and a fair share of jerseys with names on the back despite "Jeter 2" or "Mantle 7" never appearing on an actual game-issued uniform.

Late Yankees owner George Steinbrenner, who came to baseball from college football as an assistant at Northwestern and Ohio State, brought some of that gridiron mentality with him to the diamond. Uni Watch's Paul Lukas explains: "There's a whole subculture of [college] coaches who refuse to put names on the back unless the team earns it by going to a bowl game, or improving on last year's record, or whatever. It's used as a motivator. I don't think this is done so much in baseball, but the underlying principle—the team versus the individual—is the same."

Even on Opening Day, Red Sox Nation knows the identity of every Boston player in Fenway Park, despite the lack of nameplates.

BASEBALL DEFINED

Kitchen

In baseball the kitchen is not a place for a late-night snack; it's the area near the high and inside part of the strike zone, between the batter's upper hip and chest. A fastball fired into this area is especially difficult to hit and perhaps intimidating. It is a favorite term of former ballplayers in the broadcast booth, who often admonish pitchers for not throwing inside more. The term lends itself to illustrative sayings: "He got in his kitchen and broke a few dishes." Another related expression, "pots and pans," is also used when describing inside heat's effect on a batter's comfort level.

Why do some teams not have player's names on the back of their uniforms?

Thinking Man's Yaz

"I think about baseball when I wake up in the morning. I think about it all day and I dream about it at night. The only time I don't think about it is when I'm playing it."—Carl Yastrzemski, Hall of Fame outfielder

Even during batting practice before his final All-Star Game in 1982 in Montreal, Carl Yastrzemski worked tirelessly at his craft.

PHOTO CREDIT: DAN CARUBIA

Did You Know

Pinstripers

The Yankees were neither the first nor the last team to wear pinstriped uniforms, but they are the team most famous for them. The 1911 Giants were the first New York team to don pinstripes. The Yankees followed a year later, dropped the look after one season, and put on the pinstripes for good in 1915. Though it makes for a good story that the Yankees adopted the pinstripes to make Babe Ruth look slimmer, the Bambino was actually still pretty lithe when he arrived in the Bronx in 1920 and only needed the slimming illusion of vertical stripes during his beefier later years with the club. The pinstripe look has always been popular in New York. Like the Yankees, the Brooklyn Dodgers started wearing pinstripes in 1912. The Dodgers ditched the look in 1937, five years after the Giants had done the same. When the New York Mets came in to being in 1962, they jumped right in with pinstripes. Despite wearing white or black uniforms primarily in recent years, pinstripes remain the official Mets home uniform.

WHO WON THE FIRST WORLD SERIES?

The Boston Red Sox won the first World Series as we know it in 1903, but that feud-ending best-of-nine affair was not the first competition to be called a World Series. The Boston-Pittsburgh World Series came about after a compromise to end the player stealing and contract jumping running rampant between the upstart American League (established 1901) and the National League (established 1876). But the first championship played between rival leagues had been held two decades earlier.

Cincinnati won the first title of the American Association, a major league founded in 1882. They took on Cap Anson's NL champion Chicago club after the season was over. The National League did not yet recognize the new league, so all of Anson's players technically had to be released so they would be independent players for the two-game exhibition. Each team notched a shutout win against the other. No one at the time saw these as more than exhibition games and besides, it essentially ended in a tie. Two years later came the first real "World Series." (The nineteenth century version is in quotes to differentiate it from the World Series we know today.)

The American Association and National League made peace in 1884 and agreed that the NL champion Providence Grays would face the AA champion New York Mets "for the championship of the United States." The three-game set was held in New York. "Old Hoss" Radbourn, with a never-to-be-matched 59 victories to his credit that year, won three more times in a Providence sweep. The press called Radbourn's club "champions of the world" and the title was coined.

The AA St. Louis Browns played in the next four "World Series," winning the first two against Chicago before losing the next two to NL reps the Detroit Wolverines and the New York Giants, respectively. In 1889 the Giants beat the AA Brooklyn Bridegrooms, who hopped over to the NL after the season. The Bridegrooms, known today as the Dodgers, faired slightly better in their maiden season in the NL, forging a championship tie in 1890 "World Series," deadlocked with AA Louisville Cyclones, 3–3–1.

No one could know how the twentieth century version of the World Series would take hold of the public's imagination, but it got off to a good start with Cy Young throwing the first pitch in 1903. When not pitching, he even helped sell tickets for the Series at Boston's Huntington Avenue Grounds.

PHOTO CREDIT: NATIONAL BASEBALL HALL OF FAME, COOPERSTOWN, NY

Resumed fighting between the American Association and National League, brought about by the player and franchise grabbing after the demise of the one-year Players' League, resulted in no championship between leagues in 1891, the last year of the AA's decade-long run. Championship series were sporadically held between the top two NL teams through 1900. And then all hell broke loose.

The American League, formerly the minor Western League, pronounced itself a major league and direct competitor to the National League in 1901. The NL had contracted by four teams after the 1899 season and three of those vacated cities—Baltimore, Washington, and Cleveland—begat AL franchises. The new league also put teams in direct competition with the NL in Boston, Chicago, and Philadelphia, with St. Louis joining the head-to-head fight when Milwaukee relocated there in 1902. Detroit, once home to the NL champion Wolverines of 1887, was an AL hotbed in the new century.

The leagues bled each other for two years before a peace agreement was reached in 1903, with each league vowing to respect the player contracts of the other. The National League had its own internal bickering while the American League had to clean up a messy situation left by John McGraw. As manager of Baltimore's AL club, McGraw tried to run the Orioles into the ground, scheming to bring the team's best players to the NL when he hightailed it to New York to take over the Giants. Baltimore's AL franchise shifted to New York, where it became the team now known as the Yankees; it was both a strategic move and a swipe at McGraw by AL president Ban Johnson.

As the 1903 season wound down, the pennant in the new circuit was handily wrapped up by Boston's American League club, now known as the Red Sox and then called by several names, with Americans used as often as anything else. The Pittsburgh Pirates won their third straight NL pennant in 1903. The two owners came to an agreement in September to play each other after the season. The Pirates

Did You Know?

Nobody's Patsy

Patsy Dougherty was the first player in history to lead off a World Series game with a home run and the first to hit two in a Fall Classic. After the Red Sox lost the first modern World Series game to Pittsburgh in 1903, Dougherty led off the next game with a home run. He hit another in the sixth inning. It was not only a first in World Series history—and helped produce the first win by an American League club in postseason competition—but no player with fewer than 40 career homers besides Dougherty has ever hit multiple homers in one Series game. It was also the last home run by anybody for five years, a span of twenty-four World Series games. Joe Tinker was the next to go deep in the Fall Classic, for the Cubs in Game Two in 1908. In that homer unhappy era, Dougherty hit only 17 homers in 5,109 career plate appearances outside of his power day of October 2, 1903.

were seen as favorites to win the first modern World Series—the broad name of the series remained though it was strictly a national competition.

Boston's Cy Young, already with 314 career wins on his way to an untouchable 511, lost the first World Series game. Pittsburgh won three of the first four games, but Boston took the last four to capture the best-of-nine affair. Cy Young won two and Bill Dinneen the other three, complete games all. Deacon Phillippe started—and completed—five games for the Pirates, a record unmatched in modern World Series play.

Giants manager Mugsy McGraw and owner John T. Brush steadfastly refused to play a World Series in 1904 because of their dispute with Ban Johnson, denying Boston a chance to repeat in October. The Giants did play for the world championship in 1905—beating the Philadelphia Athletics to give the NL its first World Series win—and the Series continued through world wars, financial crisis, and even an earthquake. The only thing that has stopped the World Series since the McGraw-Johnson feud was a strike that erased the 1994 title bout.

The World Series has rarely had a problem attracting a crowd.

Pennant

This is one of those things that is obvious to older fans, but still should be stated for the record: In general—and in this book—a pennant is won when a team earns the right to represent its league in the World Series. The pennant itself is a meager piece of material flapping in the breeze, but since the term was first coined in 1879 it has symbolized the reward for a season of maximum effort and beating the odds. And the task keeps getting harder. There were no scheduled playoffs before 1969, so a team clinched the pennant during the regular season. Since 1969 a pennant required winning the League Championship Series. Starting in 1995—plus a one-year exception during strike-torn 1981—victory in a Division Series and the LCS became the path to the pennant.

QUOTABLE

One Precinct Reporting

"If the World Series runs until election day, the networks will run the first one-half inning and project the winner."
—Lindsey Nelson, broadcaster

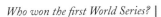

Who won the first World Series? |

JUST WHAT IS A
SANDLOT ANYWAY?

The sandlot is a concept from days gone by. Simply put, a sandlot is a vacant, usually grassless, lot where kids play baseball on their own while mastering the intricacies, difficulties, and love of the game through repetition, competition, and bonding. Baseball with no uniforms and no grownups.

The classic image of the sandlot kid goes back to the nineteenth century: a boy standing in coveralls, barefoot, holding a homemade bat, and waiting for a pitch. That is the pose in Victor Salvatore's bronze sculpture "Sandlot Kid" that stands in front of Doubleday Field in Cooperstown, New York. The sculpture has been on display since the Hall of Fame opened in 1939.

Author Peter Tamony traced the term sandlot back to 1850 in San Francisco. By the turn of the century it was often used in conjunction with kids playing baseball. Sandlot remains a generic term that can mean anything from neighborhood kids playing pickup baseball to loosely affiliated youth leagues. The proceeds from the Mayor's Trophy Games in New York between the Dodgers and Yankees in the 1940s and 1950s went to "New York sandlot baseball," with the two major league clubs fielding requests from area teams soliciting funds for equipment. There was a similar arrangement for the annual exhibition by the same name played by the Mets and Yankees in the 1960s, 1970s, and early 1980s.

The sandlot is now more a piece of nostalgia than a place where kids actually go on their own, choose up sides, and play until it gets too dark to hit. Organized youth sports, travel teams, fall ball, and even year-round baseball in warmer climates are now the norm. If there is time, kids playing on their own are probably more likely to play Wiffle ball, or in urban areas—and this really may be a stretch nowadays—taking to the streets for a game of stickball or one of its derivatives played with a stoop or hand.

Some will cite parental insistence on control, the need to know where their children are 24 hours a day. Safety for children is of course crucial, but the alternative to sandlots in many cases has simply meant keeping kids in the backyard or indoors. The lack of spontaneity has eroded the casual nature of the pickup sandlot game, where whoever comes to the sandlot gets to play, the teams and ground rules constantly changing. When there weren't enough players, for example, hitting to right field became an automatic out because there was no right fielder. Cleon Jones, an All-Star for the 1969 "Miracle Mets" was a natural lefty who reached the major leagues throwing left but batting right because when he was a kid, if he hit left-handed in the sandlot near his home in Mobile, Alabama, the odds were that Cleon would launch one into the river and lose the only ball they had.

Blame for the decline in sandlot baseball also rests with kids. Fascination, obsession even, with electronics or the latest computer games often trumps the desire to be out on a makeshift diamond playing with large groups of kids, where not everyone might be a friend—at least for the first half dozen games on the day. Drive through a few towns on a summer afternoon and you will pass by perfectly manicured baseball fields sitting unused.

Most kids now know of the sandlot only as a movie. The 1993 film *The Sandlot* (and its two sequels) focused on a vacant area in the neighborhood where kids called the shots, had a good time, and in the end, did the right thing. Set in California in the early 1960s, when baseball was still the country's favorite sport, one of the original film's best and truest lines is advice from the sandlot's top player to a novice trying to fit into a new town by learning the game: "Man, this is baseball. You gotta stop thinking. Just have fun."

The sandlot is still alive and kicking. It's just located in Latin America, where equipment is often scarce and the only grownups are the various scouts who occasionally stop by looking for the next Jose Reyes or Hanley Ramirez to bring to one of the baseball academies in Venezuela and the Dominican Republic. Former major league catcher and sandlot advocate Brent Mayne did the math and figured that a kid playing sandlot baseball in the Dominican can get almost eight times more at bats in a month than an American youth playing three organized games per week. And the sandlotter does so

Kids made their own rules and teams during 2010 Sandlot Day in several states. In Philipsburg, New York, the only adult help the kids needed was in making a sign . . . and getting everyone together for a picture.

"without the wear and tear of playing under pressure and the risk of burn out," Mayne said. "Should we be surprised that the best players in the world come from a tiny little island?"

There is still hope for the vanishing sandlot in the United States. A handful of towns have set up summer programs for baseball where kids run the show. Other towns are taking part in a new movement called Sandlot Day to put kids back in charge of the fields and leave the parents at home. It was held in 2010 at no cost in several towns, mostly in New York, with an organizing theme of . . . no organization. Just like the "good old days," the kids make the decisions and

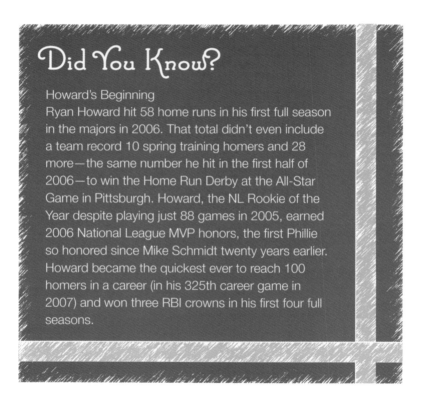

Did You Know?

Howard's Beginning

Ryan Howard hit 58 home runs in his first full season in the majors in 2006. That total didn't even include a team record 10 spring training homers and 28 more—the same number he hit in the first half of 2006—to win the Home Run Derby at the All-Star Game in Pittsburgh. Howard, the NL Rookie of the Year despite playing just 88 games in 2005, earned 2006 National League MVP honors, the first Phillie so honored since Mike Schmidt twenty years earlier. Howard became the quickest ever to reach 100 homers in a career (in his 325th career game in 2007) and won three RBI crowns in his first four full seasons.

pick their own managers, captains, and umpires. Kids from different leagues play on the same field. Problems are worked out by the kids, which is probably as big a lesson as learning to handle a hot grounder at third base. Every ruling on Sandlot Day may not have been fair, but life isn't always so. That it took a three-page memo from the Youth Sports Institute to get parents to understand the concept shows how far we've drifted from the sandlot. But that it was written up in the *New York Times* and deemed a success by the majority of participants shows that the sandlot still could make a comeback.

PHOTO CREDIT: SHUTTERSTOCK IMAGES

Phillies slugger Ryan Howard puts everything into every swing and could hit a ball 400 feet before he was even a teenager.

Pepper

About all that remains of this fast-paced game of catch and hit at close range are the signs reading NO PEPPER GAMES at stadiums. But those signs have worn away or the ballparks they graced have been torn down, so all that actually remains of pepper is the memory of its prohibition. Pepper was a fast-moving game where a handful of players threw to a batter some 30 feet or less away; the batter hit their offerings back at them hard, despite swinging without breaking the wrists. Concern about damaging the fields and the customers in the expensive seats are reasons given for pepper's suppression and demise on the major league level.

QUOTABLE

No Sugarcoating Lemon

"Baseball was made for kids, and grown-ups only screw it up." — Bob Lemon, Hall of Fame pitcher

WHY IS THERE A SEVENTH-INNING STRETCH?

There are many explanations for how the seventh-inning stretch began, but the why of the seventh-inning stretch rings true in all the tales: By the seventh inning the body gets tired of sitting. It's not a problem of having shorter attention spans or larger bodies than our forebears—even fans of the first professional team got fidgety by the time the middle of the seventh inning rolled around.

Harry Wright, manager of the Cincinnati Red Stockings, noticed that jogging in from his center field position in 1869, "That spectators all arise between halves of the seventh inning, extend their legs and arms and sometimes walk about," Wright wrote to a friend. "In so doing they enjoy the relief afforded by relaxation from a long posture upon hard benches."

Hard wooden seats seem to be a recurring theme for making spectators want to stand after 90 minutes or so. The hard benches even softened Jesuit discipline at the ballpark. Students flocked to Manhattan College home games in the 1880s, often played at the nearby Polo Grounds, but they were under the watchful eye of Brother Jasper, who served as both coach and prefect of discipline (as well as source of the college's nickname, the Jaspers). A Manhattan College version of events on file at the National Baseball Hall of Fame Library in Cooperstown stated that before each game Brother Jasper "sharply admonished the students not to leave their seats or move about until the game was over and they were ready to return to the college for the evening meal. Then, the good Brother went down to the bench and directed the play of the team."

On an oppressively hot day in a drawn-out 1882 game, Brother Jasper noticed the students getting restless. "So as the team came to bat in the seventh inning, he went over to the stands and told his charges to stand, stretch, and move about for a minute or two. This eased the tension and unrest, and so Brother Jasper repeated it in the next few games." That 1882 game was reportedly against

Pickle

Pickle is what a runner finds himself in when he is caught in a rundown between bases. Pickle is also the name given to a childhood game sometimes called "running bases," where two kids throw a ball back and forth and a runner tries to beat the tag. If someone beats the play, he or she usually becomes a fielder and the player who missed the ball or the tag becomes a runner. The game teaches runners to think while caught in an unenviable situation on the bases and fielders to act coolly and execute when a seeming sure out presents itself in a game situation.

the Metropolitans, a semi-professional team at the time, that called the Polo Grounds home. This "standing tradition" later passed to supporters of the New York Giants. Yet seventh-inning stretch observations in the recorded history of the game lag for almost thirty years, when a sitting U.S. President decided to stand.

William Howard Taft was an enormous fan of baseball; and the adjective could describe the twenty-seventh president himself. Weighing in at more than 300 pounds, he was the heaviest commander in chief in history (though he dropped 80 pounds after leaving office in 1913). Taft was the first chief executive to take an interest in baseball, becoming the first president to throw out a first pitch. In 1910 he began, or more accurately, renewed a tradition that had its roots four decades earlier. In the middle of the seventh inning, President Taft freed himself from the constraints of a wooden seat that had to be growing uncomfortable against his frame. As he stood, the crowd rose out of respect.

Being a president has its advantages. Though the one-termer Taft is the only person to serve as both president and chief justice of the Supreme Court—and was the last president with facial hair— most people today are as likely to remember his popularization

𝒟id 𝒴ou 𝒦now?

Just Plain Daffy

The Daffiness Boys originated in Brooklyn, referring to the club's pranksters and clowns, specifically two different teams over two decades. Originally coined for Wilbert Robinson's Brooklyn club in the 1920s, the easy-going manager was dubbed Uncle Robbie and his team was known as the Robins. The Daffiness Boys handle stuck after some bizarre incidents occurred on the field with the likes of Dazzy Vance, Chick Fewster, and Babe Herman. In 1926 it happened that all three players wound up on third base on Herman's hit—the unforgettable doubling into a double play (tripling into a triple play sounds even funnier but isn't quite accurate). Things were still a little daffy in Brooklyn by the time Casey Stengel landed his first major league managing job there in 1934, but by then the Daffiness Boys had another charter in St. Louis: Jay Hanna "Dizzy" Dean and Paul Dee "Daffy" Dean, fraternal mound leaders of the Gashouse Gang. Those Daffy Cards were world champions in '34. Another wacky bird, Daffy Duck, began a new era of daffiness when he debuted in cartoon form in '37.

President William Howard Taft stood up in the seventh inning and all followed.

of the seventh-inning stretch than any of his policies. Nowadays songs are sung, T-shirts launched, sausages raced, and even likenesses of presidents vie for the finish line at games in Washington (William Howard Taft's likeness is markedly absent), but the one universal event that happens at professional ballgames throughout the United States, Canada, Japan, Latin America, and elsewhere is that everyone stands between the top and the bottom of the seventh inning. Stretching, singing, and sausage racing are optional.

Before they went "live" in Milwaukee the day Robin Yount's number was retired in 1994, the fabled sausage race had its origins on the County Stadium scoreboard. Go, brat, go!

QUOTABLE

It is Called a Pastime

"The strongest thing that baseball has going for it today are its yesterdays." —Lawrence Ritter, writer

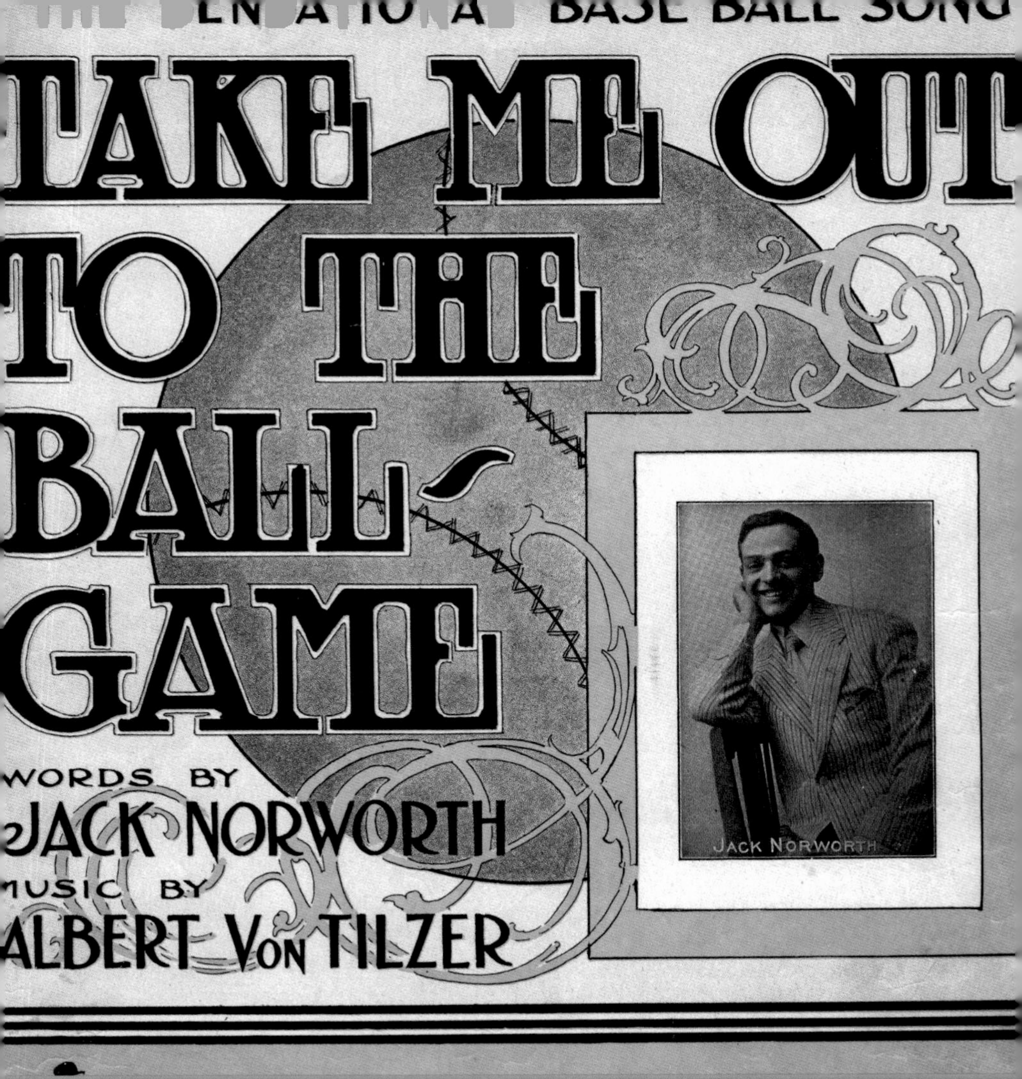

WHO WROTE "TAKE ME OUT TO THE BALL GAME"?

Jack Norworth, a vaudeville performer, knew next to nothing about baseball, but he certainly knew how to create a memorable little ditty. In 1908, a year in which baseball fever gripped much of the nation, and New York in particular, Norworth was standing on a subway platform when he saw a sign that proclaimed: "Baseball Today—Polo Grounds." While others around him made plans to see the New York Giants play in Upper Manhattan, Norworth took a scrap of paper and started writing down plans for a date with Katie Casey, who later became Nelly Kelly. Whatever her name, she was baseball mad.

As Norworth wrote, he conjured the young female baseball fanatic being asked by her beau to take in a show on a Saturday. She said no, but she did tell her suitor the one place she longed to go. Norworth then penned eight of the most memorable lines in the history of American song, known by heart by people from the first decade of two different centuries and all the years in between. It is known by children who can barely speak and even by grownups who, like Norworth, had never even been to a game. It was set to music by Albert Von Tilzer and published by York Music, and the chorus was memorable from the start:

> **Take me out to the ball game,**
> **Take me out with the crowd;**
> **Buy me some peanuts and Cracker Jack,**
> **I don't care if I never get back.**
> **Let me root, root, root for the home team,**
> **If they don't win it's a shame.**
> **For it's one, two, three strikes you're out,**
> **At the old ball game.**

Yet the song wasn't a big hit initially. It took a New York baseball tragedy—Merkle's Boner—to heighten the baseball senses. Fred Merkle failed to touch second base as the deciding run scored against the Cubs on September 23, 1908, and as the fans poured on the field after the apparent game-winning hit, the Cubs retrieved a ball, stepped on the base, and umpire Hank O'Day called Merkle out even as the field became unplayable with all the commotion. After the resulting brouhaha, the teams were even in the standings, and when the regular season ended, the tie was replayed. The Cubs won the rematch. The Tigers came out on top of a tight American League race. Even though Chicago's subsequent five-game victory over Detroit was a dud of a World Series, baseball fever was rampant. When Billy Murray recorded Norworth and Von Tilzer's song in late October, "Take Me Out to the Ball Game" became an overnight sensation. The two verses sung about Katie or Kelly or whatever you want to call her, are pretty much forgotten. But no one can forget the chorus.

It is still the third-most sung tune in the United States, trailing only "Happy Birthday" and "The Star-Spangled Banner." According to Tim Wiles, coauthor of *Baseball's Greatest Hit*, "Take Me Out to the Ball Game" has been covered by 600 different artists, a diverse lineup that includes Bing Crosby, the Andrews Sisters, Frank Sinatra, LL Cool J, Aretha Franklin, Liberace, Jimmy Buffett, Bob Dylan, and the Goo Goo Dolls. Add in a strong bench with instrumental versions by the Boston Pops, Harpo Marx, and Billy Joel.

The song has been featured in 1,200 movies and it's even been sung in protest. A sports radio station in Kent, Ohio, played the song 25,000 times in a row as a far-from-silent protest over the 1994 baseball strike. In major league ballparks alone, "Take Me Out to the Ball Game" is sung more than 5,000 times annually.

During the 1970s some parks played organ versions of the tune at various times during games. Announcer Harry Caray starting singing it to himself in the Chicago White Sox booth—and owner Bill Veeck noticed the fans near the booth were singing along with him at a game in 1976—so a mike was secretly planted the next day. The song's popularity, not to mention Caray's, received a full-throated boost. Caray was proof to everyone that you didn't have to be an Irish tenor to sing the song, you just had to belt it out. And everyone

did. Caray brought the tradition with him when he moved across
town to the Cubs. In memory of Caray, who died in 1998, the Cubs
still invite a different person up to the booth to sing the song during
the seventh inning at Wrigley Field. Stadiums throughout baseball
play the song and often include the words on the scoreboard—just
in case there's someone in attendance who might not already know
them.

Shaw at the Show

"What is both surprising and delightful is that spectators are allowed, and even expected, to join in the vocal part of the game . . . There is no reason why the field should not try to put the batsman off his stroke at the critical moment by neatly timed disparagements of his wife's fidelity and his mother's respectability."—George Bernard Shaw, playwright

Tim Wiles explains that Jack Norworth, who claimed he wrote "3,000 songs, seven of them good," probably concocted the story about "Take Me Out to the Ballgame" coming to him while looking at the placard on the subway and his having never been to a game until 1940. "These claims, none of which were made prior to Albert Von Tilzer's death in 1956, were promulgated by Norworth in 1958 to promote the song on its fiftieth anniversary," Wiles explained.

Announcer Harry Caray, who made "Take Me Out to the Ballgame" even more famous, remains forever in mid-chorus outside Wrigley Field. "A one, a two, a three…"

PHOTO CREDIT: AL YELLON/
BLEEDCUBBIEBLUE.COM

Ribeye Steaks

Another in a long line of food items turned into baseball jargon, this is the most mouthwatering to hitters. Run batted in, shortened to RBI, gets pronounced ribbie for fun, and then sizzles into a ribeye steak when an announcer gets hold of it. The term is a favorite of Mets announcer Keith Hernandez, who had a 1,071 such meals during seventeen seasons in the big leagues.

A century and counting after he penned his greatest hit—and we're not talking about "Shine on Harvest Moon"—it's hard to fault the old vaudevillian for milking his trot around the bases. It's not like anyone's going to stop singing.

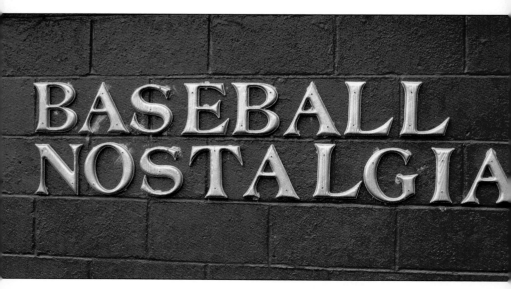

A sign in Cooperstown tells what the store—and the town—is offering.

HOW MANY TIMES DID
TY COBB STEAL HOME?

Ty Cobb stole home 54 times during his career, far more than anyone else in history. Like Cy Young's 511 wins, it is a record that will probably never be approached.

Those 54 steals meant 54 runs accounted for by Cobb himself. During much of his career, offense was at a premium. And given that Cobb, who was also the American League's best hitter, was already on base, the chances of another Detroit Tiger knocking him home were slimmer than if Cobb, also one of the most prolific run producers ever, was at the plate. So Cobb took the matter into his own hands—or feet. The Georgia Peach tearing for home with his sharp spikes rendered a catcher's primitive shin pads and chest protector as useless as a suit of armor trying to stop a bullet.

Cobb stole 892 bases during his career, a record that stood for nearly half a century. He now ranks third to Rickey Henderson's 1,406 steals (with just four career swipes of home). Other Cobb records have been surpassed through the years: 3,034 games played (he now ranks fifth), 11,434 at bats (fifth), 2,246 runs (second), 4,189 hits

The corner of Michigan and Trumbull Avenues was Ty Cobb's home for eighteen years. You couldn't walk into Tiger Stadium without knowing that it had once been the lair of the greatest Tiger of them all, "A Genius in Spikes."

(second), 5,854 total bases (fifth), 2,213 RBIs (seventh), and 1,135 extra-base hits (eleventh). A discrepancy in the records resulted in two hits (which erroneously had been recorded twice) being subtracted from Cobb's 1910 total, and lowered his all-time batting average to .366—though the evidence wasn't found until after Cobb's death. That was fortunate, because taking away anything Cobb achieved on the field was taking your life in your hands (see definition, page 153).

Tyrus Raymond Cobb made his debut in Detroit in 1905 at age 18, the youngest player in the majors. He seethed at being razzed by the veterans and hit just .240. After an illness shortened his second season, he never again batted below .324 until his final year—when he hit .323 at age 41. In between Cobb won a record 12 batting titles—11, if you consider that the hit total discrepancy found by Pete Palmer in 1981 resulted in the contentious 1910 batting crown going to Cleveland's Napoleon Lajoie. (That change in Cobb's career hit total also meant that Pete Rose actually broke Cobb's all-time hit mark two games *before* it was celebrated so ardently in Cincinnati in 1985.)

An irascible man on his best day, Cobb was hated by opponents and teammates alike, but his fellow Tigers didn't mind having him in the lineup. After he jumped into the crowd to beat up a handi-capped New York heckler in 1912, Cobb's teammates reacted to his indefinite suspension by refusing to play a game in Philadelphia. The Tigers grabbed several local pickup players to stand in and lost to the Athletics 24–2. Cobb thanked his teammates and urged them to return to the field. Cobb served a ten-game suspension and paid a $50 fine. He still wound up hitting .400 for the second straight year, the only American league player to ever do so. He hit .400 a third time ten years later. By then he was player-manager in Detroit. He was not any better liked as a manager. His Tigers had winning records but were generally second division (see definition, page 153).

Tris Speaker, the only player in history with more doubles and outfield assists than Cobb, was implicated in a gambling scandal with Cobb and pitcher turned outfielder "Smoky" Joe Wood. Though the scandal was made public in the winter of 1927, it dated back to a game late in the 1919 season. AL president Ban Johnson insisted that Speaker and Cobb resign as managers. Both did, but they were subsequently exonerated by commissioner Kenesaw Mountain Landis. Cobb signed a lucrative deal to play for the Athletics in 1927 and Speaker joined the Senators. Johnson was subsequently forced out as league president. Cobb rapped the 4,000th hit of his career for Philadelphia, retiring a year before the A's won the 1929 World Series. Though the Tigers won three straight pennants in his first five seasons with the club, Cobb never won a world championship—about the only hardware he did not collect in his career.

He was in the first class of inductees into the Hall of Fame, receiving 222 out of 226 votes, more than contemporaries Babe Ruth, Walter Johnson, Honus Wagner, and Christy Mathewson. As shrewd as he was mean, Cobb amassed a fortune—much of it thanks to his investment in a local Georgia company called Coca-Cola. He died at age 74 in 1961.

That's all fine, you say, but what about those steals of home? Let's take a look at the information, as provided by Baseball Almanac. (Note that he did not steal home in 1905, 1906, and 1925.)

Year	Steals of Home	Stolen Solo	Double Steal	Triple Steal
1907	2	0	2	0
1908	3	0	3	0
1909	3	1	2	0
1910	3	3	0	0
1911	5	1	3	1
1912	8	2	6	0
1913	4	3	1	0
1914	1	0	1	0
1915	5	3	0	2
1916	1	1	0	0
1917	1	1	0	0
1918	1	0	1	0

1919	1	0	0	1
1920	3	2	1	0
1921	2	1	1	0
1922	2	1	1	0
1923	1	0	1	0
1924	3	0	1	0
1926	1	1	0	0
1927	3	0	1	2
1928	1	1	0	0
Total	**54**	**23**	**25**	**6**

Of Cobb's 54 steals of home during his career, 23 came with no trail runners. A triple steal, one of baseball's rarest plays today, accounted for six of his thefts of home. A double steal, the most popular way for players to steal home when they dare try nowadays, accounted for 25 of Cobb's total. His eight steals of home in 1912—the same year he was suspended for 10 games—is still the most in major league history, though Rod Carew swiped home seven times in 1969 (Carew had 17 home thefts in his career). Cobb did not steal home in either of his first two seasons in

Ty Cobb. Picture perfect . . . on the field, that is.

Did You Know?

Bloom off the Rose
During his chase of Ty Cobb's all-time hits record, Pete Rose endured two streaks of more than 1,000 at bats without a home run in the 1980s. He is one of just a handful of position players to ever have multiple four-digit at bat droughts without a homer. The first baseman went homerless in 1981, 1983, 1984, and 1986. The Reds player-manager did hit two home runs in 1985, the year he surpassed Cobb's career hit mark. The 44-year-old Rose's "backup" that season at first base was 43-year-old Tony Perez, like Rose a cog in the Big Red Machine of the 1970s.

Ty Cobb's plaque is front and center of the first class at the Hall of Fame. To the left: Christy Mathewson (above) and Babe Ruth. To the right: Honus Wagner and Walter Johnson.

Second Division

A euphemism for a team with no chance of winning the pennant. Back when both leagues had eight teams apiece, second division referred to the clubs from fifth place on down, or sixth place to the bottom when the leagues expanded to ten teams each in the 1960s. Usage dates back to the early 1900s, but by the 1970s the term became obsolete as both leagues broke into divisions. Old-timers and people fancying arcane terms still use it. No matter what division you're in, it still means you're just playing out the string.

the majors, but he swiped home at least once in 21 of his final 22 seasons, coming up empty only in 1925. In addition, he stole his way around the bases—swiping second, third, and home in the same inning—four times in his career. Surprisingly, Cobb is not among the eleven players who have stolen home twice in the same game.

Max Carey set the National League record with 33 career steals of home, but no one was in the same league as Ty Cobb.

QUOTABLE

This Explains a Lot

"When I began playing the game, baseball was about as gentlemanly as a kick in the crotch."—Ty Cobb, Hall of Fame outfielder

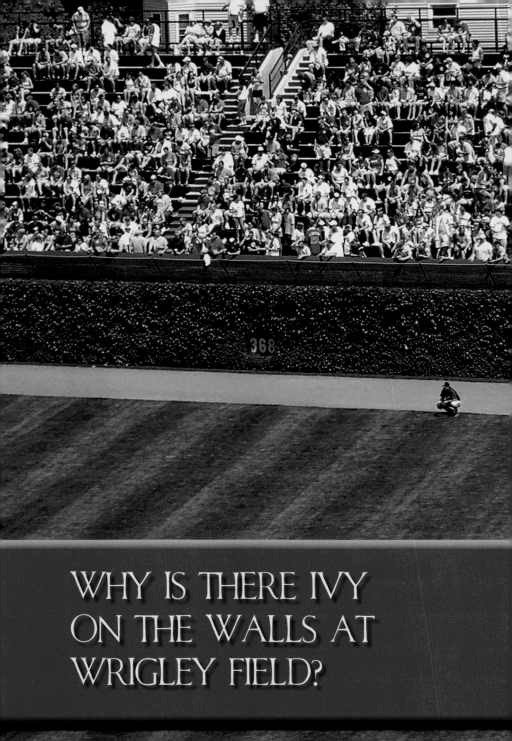

WHY IS THERE IVY
ON THE WALLS AT
WRIGLEY FIELD?

I vy on a wall is a beautiful thing to behold. It looks so stately on the wall at a baseball stadium that even a few recent ballparks have let it grow on batter's eyes in center field, but there is only one place where ivy is a star: Wrigley Field.

The ivy is the sparkle in the diamond jewel on Chicago's North Side. While everything about the venerable park—except the bathrooms—is worthy of being embraced by fans, the ivy is what it all comes back to. With no padding on the walls, the ivy is as close as an outfielder gets to protection when taking on the brick wall. It invokes a ground rule when the ball rolls into it, with the pursuing outfielder putting up his hands in a sign of mock surrender. It is the ivy that separates these same outfielders from their adoring fans or tormentors, depending on the color of one's uniform. The ivy is what makes the confines of Wrigley friendly. The ivy is what keeps the place full of people even though the Cubs haven't won a world championship since its founding. And it was built in 1914.

Wrigley Field was not even built for the Cubs. It was built by restaurant mogul Charley Weeghman for Chicago's third team, an entry in the short-lived Federal League. According to Stuart Shea, author of *Wrigley Field: The Unauthorized Biography*, the third major league's opening crowd in Chicago on April 23, 1914, saw a celebration worthy of the multitudes that would follow in the decades to come: "Soldiers fired a 21-gun salute, and the club set off a barrage of fireworks when the flag reached the top of the flag pole." Flowers and gifts were presented to Chi-Fed manager Joe Tinker, the former Cubs shortstop of twin-killing fame. The walls, however, were simple uncovered brick.

The Chi-Feds—they took the name Whales their second season—had a better record than the Cubs in both 1914 and 1915. After finishing a close second their inaugural year, the Whales won the closest race in major league history the following season: a mere .0009 percentage points ahead of the St. Louis Terriers and .0037 better than the Pittsburgh Rebels. Chicago and Pittsburgh didn't play the full schedule due to rainouts, but the financially strapped

Wrigley Field in the 2000s looks much as it did in the 1930s and even retains the feel from its Federal League roots of 1914.

league wasn't in a position to schedule makeups. Chicago was declared champion after splitting a season-ending doubleheader with Pittsburgh, the overflow crowd indulged in "one of the biggest cushion fights ever staged in a Chicago ball park," according to the newspapers.

When the league folded, the owners of the Federal League clubs in Chicago and St. Louis were allowed to buy the Cubs and Browns, respectively. Most of the other Fed owners got a small settlement from the two major leagues; some got nothing. The Federal League was soon forgotten, except in Chicago, where the Cubs moved into beautiful Weeghman Park.

The Cubs won a pennant for Weeghman, again in a shortened schedule. Due to World War I, the major leagues shut down after Labor Day in 1918. The Cubs won the pennant, but the park was denied its first World Series because the home games were transferred to larger Comiskey Park. The Cubs lost to Babe Ruth's Red Sox in what would be Boston's last world championship for 86 years.

The war and the influenza epidemic hurt restaurants but not gum, so confectionary magnate William Wrigley Jr. bought out Weeghman in the wake of the 1918 pennant—and the armistice in Europe. When Wrigley invited several sportswriters to dinner near his California home, Bill Veeck Sr., sportswriter for the *Chicago American*, told Wrigley how poorly the team was being run. Wrigley made Veeck chew on his own words and hired him as vice president. He ascended to the club's presidency by July 1919.

Bill Veeck Sr. is not the Bill Veeck who's in the Hall of Fame, though the Cubs did employ Bill Veeck Jr., his first step toward his fabled career as a baseball executive. Bill Sr. was running the show as the Cubs won pennants in 1929 and 1932. Though Bill Sr. died of leukemia in 1933, the younger Veeck remained with the Cubs and eventually rose to treasurer before going into ownership elsewhere.

Bill Veeck Jr. headed up the Wrigley expansion project that created the bleachers as we know them in 1937, but his Cubs legacy is the ivy. The park's telltale feature was planted twenty-three years after the ballpark was built. The idea came from Philip K. Wrigley, whose family name was put on the park in 1926 (the same name as the minor league park built in Los Angeles the previous year). The younger Wrigley constantly pushed "beautiful Wrigley Field" as a concept and a goal. Keep in mind, however, that P. K. also thought his plan for the "College of Coaches," a revolving door of coaches managing the team in the 1960s, was a good idea. It wasn't. The ivy, now that was genius.

And here's the kick—it wasn't really ivy. P. K. Wrigley wanted it done before the 1937 season ended so his friends could see the ballpark improvements, but ivy grows slowly. As he would do throughout his life, Veeck improvised and it couldn't have turned out better.

Clavey Nursery in suburban Woodstock suggested a quick-growing Japanese vine called bittersweet, which would impress P. K.'s pals. So Veeck, groundskeeper Don Knorr, Gordon Clavey, and a handful of others set to work in September 1937 and planted 350 bittersweet plants on the wall and interspersed 200 ivy plants, which eventually became the dominant plant. The type of ivy is known as Boston ivy, for those interested in gardening or irony.

While young Gordon Clavey would become president of the family nursery, Bill Veeck Jr. likewise joined the family business. But it wasn't in Chicago. Not yet, at least. After running the minor league Milwaukee Brewers and being severely wounded while serving in the South Pacific in World War II (he eventually lost his right leg), Veeck

Did You Know?

Travel Restricted Area
World War II greatly affected the way the baseball was played; not just in terms of who played it, but where it was played and when. While Washington wanted more night games to keep military and civilian war industry personnel entertained after work, the Cubs scrapped their planned lights—literally—and donated the material to the war effort (Wrigley Field did not install lights until 1988). The 1945 All-Star Game was cancelled due to travel restrictions, a state of affairs that also altered home field advantage in two World Series. To lessen travel and save resources for the war effort, the traditional setup of the World Series—two games in one city, three games in the opponent's city, and two games back at the original site—was changed. In 1943 and 1945 the American League hosted the first three games and the National League held the last four. In both cases, the AL won: the 1943 Yankees beat the Cardinals in five games while the 1945 Tigers defeated the Cubs in seven games. The 2–3–2 format did, however, remain intact for the 1944 World Series— there were no train rides to worry about since the St. Louis Browns and Cardinals shared the same stadium. The Redbirds beat the Browns in six games.

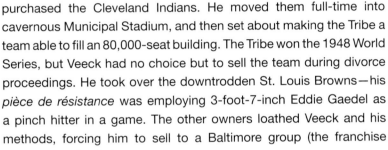

Swinging Bunt

A swinging bunt is a full swing that produces the same effect as a bunt. The batter does not generally try a swinging bunt on purpose; in a perfect situation the ball travels just as a well-placed bunt would and results in a hit—or requires a superb defensive play to prevent one.

purchased the Cleveland Indians. He moved them full-time into cavernous Municipal Stadium, and then set about making the Tribe a team able to fill an 80,000-seat building. The Tribe won the 1948 World Series, but Veeck had no choice but to sell the team during divorce proceedings. He took over the downtrodden St. Louis Browns—his *pièce de résistance* was employing 3-foot-7-inch Eddie Gaedel as a pinch hitter in a game. The other owners loathed Veeck and his methods, forcing him to sell to a Baltimore group (the franchise became the Orioles).

Veeck returned to his native Chicago—with the White Sox. The ChiSox immediately won their first pennant in forty years. He sold the team two years later due to ill health, but he purchased them again in 1975. His Pale Hose encore included surreptitiously putting Harry

The ivy at Wrigley Field is such a part of the Cubs, it sometimes even climbs off the wall and follows the club on the road. The only lights are a smile.

Carey's singing of "Take Me Out to the Ball Game" on the Comiskey Park public address system, having the already hideously clad Sox don shorts for one game, and bringing back Minnie Minoso at age 50 in 1976 so he could play in four decades—Minnie made it five decades in 1980. Disco Demolition Night was an epic disaster and he sold the club months before the 1981 strike. Veeck was through with ownership.

Veeck went back to the North Side—as a fan. He spent many afternoons during his final years in the bleachers at Wrigley Field, seated above the ivy he'd planted.

QUOTABLE

No Better Place

"Every player should be accorded the privilege of at least one season with the Chicago Cubs. That's baseball as it should be played—in God's own sunshine. And that's really living."
—Alvin Dark, Cubs third baseman (1958–59)

Any discussion of Wrigley Field has to include Ernie Banks, seen here as he was in 1969. Mr. Cub is still arguably the best player in club history. The happiest? No one's ever argued that.

WHY IS FENWAY PARK'S "GREEN MONSTER" SO TALL?

Fenway Park comes from a time when ballparks were built in the middle of cities on available and affordable land, and then the field was configured accordingly. New ballparks tend toward built-in quirks for the sake of amusement: Tal's Hill and the Crawford Boxes at Minute Maid Park in Houston, the overhanging deck in right at Citi Field, the 23-foot high right field wall made of several different surfaces at the Twins new Target Field, and other oddities scattered through the nearly two dozen parks that have opened since 1992.

There are even two minor league parks with fences that match Fenway's Green Monster: the 37-foot high replica at Hadlock Field in Portland, Maine, home of the Red Sox's Double-A affiliate; and the Arch Nemesis in York, Pennsylvania, which is six inches taller than Fenway's signature wall. As in Boston, space limitations in left field necessitated building a tall fence so batters would have to get the ball well airborne for a home run. What they lack in real estate, they make up for in height.

There certainly was nothing small about Fenway Park's predecessor, except for the seating capacity. Huntington Avenue Grounds hosted the first decade of Boston Red Sox baseball. It saw two pennants, the first modern World Series, a perfect game by Cy Young, and the transfer of the Red Stockings name—along with the allegiance of the city's baseball-loving soul—from the National League to the American League. The place barely sat 10,000; when it was absolutely jammed, they could squeeze in close to 18,000 by letting fans stand on the field—as they did during the 1903 World Series. The club wanted to accommodate more people more comfortably while also not having to endure smoke billowing in from the nearby train yard. There was room enough for a train depot in center field, which measured more than 600 feet in the early days of Huntington Avenue Grounds.

Even a century ago, land in Boston was hard to come by, but a piece of reclaimed swampland was available about a mile from the Huntington Avenue Grounds. The new ballpark was completed in time for Opening Day in 1912 at a cost of $650,000. After two days of rain, Boston's new park opened for business the same day as Detroit's rebuilt Navin Field (later called Tiger Stadium). The eleven-inning Red Sox victory over the New York Highlanders had to fight for newspaper space with the sinking of the Titanic. Fenway Park—so called for the area's marshes, or fens—was open for business.

The ballpark has undergone many changes since 1912, but Fenway Park always had a tall fence in left field because of an adjoining street and railroad tracks just beyond it. The original 25-foot wall was covered with billboards and faced a cliff, which was actually an incline caused by the low field and the height of Landsdowne Street behind it. "Duffy's Cliff" was manned by Red Sox left fielder Duffy Lewis, part of "the Million Dollar Outfield" of Lewis in left, Tris Speaker in center, and Harry Hooper in right. The dollar figure was a bit of hyperbole—the trio was later sold off for in separate deals for $70,000 plus several dispensable players—but the trio's value on the field was immeasurable. Besides providing outstanding defense, they accumulated 90 steals, batted .303 (Speaker carried the load at .383), knocked out 160 extra-base hits, knocked in 252, and scored 319 of Boston's 800 runs the year Fenway opened. On the mound, "Smoky" Joe Wood won 34 times, including 16 in a row to tie Walter Johnson's record—and beat the Big Train in a legendary showdown—as the Red Sox set a still-unparalleled team mark with 105 wins and a .691 winning percentage. They broke in the ballyard with one of the greatest World Series ever played, winning in eight games (Boston rallied in the tenth to tie Game 2 before it was called by darkness), and the Red Sox scored twice off the luckless Giants in the tenth inning to win the deciding game.

Three more world championships quickly followed, Babe Ruth came and—tragically—went, the team became a 1920s doormat, and the Red Sox were purchased by Tom Yawkey, who used his vast wealth to import stars to Fenway. The new owner also invested in the ballpark, enforcing the place in steel and concrete two decades after it had originally been built. A 37-foot high, 240-foot long fence was built of tin applied to a framework of wooden railroad ties upon a concrete base. Left field, former site of "Duffy's Cliff" was pounded out to be on the level, or at least closer to it. Left field was still just 310 feet from home plate. Center field was also made cozier—at 420 feet. Previously center field had been a limitless prairie like its Huntington Avenue predecessor, 550 feet (and farther!) from home plate. The confluence of old and new grandstands created Fenway's fabled "triangle" in center field, which became even trickier after the bullpens were moved to right field—reining in the home run distance—in 1940 (not coincidentally, the year *after* lefty-swinging Ted Williams's stunning debut).

The wall that is etched in so many imaginations in New England and beyond was covered in advertisements until 1947, when it was painted green. Coke bottles were erected above the wall fifty years later, followed by the insanely popular Green Monster seating. The wall is listed as 310 feet from home plate, but skeptics say it's closer to 305 feet.

In the wake of the world falling in love again with Fenway—and baseball—after the remarkable 1975 World Series, the stadium underwent another renovation just before Tom Yawkey died. The tin on the wall was replaced with a hard plastic coating that dents just like the tin when a ball is hit hard enough against it. The short-yet-tall fence has probably psyched enough right-handed hitters into trying to go deep—and popping up or striking out instead; so the wall has helped its fair share of hurlers through the years (though it likewise has psyched out quite a few pitchers as well). We'll let Bill Nowlin,

It wasn't so long ago that serious consideration was given to scrapping the old ballyard. Long live Fenway.

Did You Know?

It's Gone

In 2007 the all-time home run record fell to Barry Bonds with a groan. The Giants slugger had broken a cherished record, but many did not like how the aloof slugger went about it, especially given the many questions about possible steroid use by a man pursuing one of the game's most prized records. The slugger who held the record longer than Hank Aaron or Mark McGwire was none other than . . . Roger Connor. A giant for his day at 6 feet 3 inches, 220 pounds, he was a Giant when the name was coined and ended his career in 1897 with 138 major league home runs. Connor began his career in upstate New York with the NL's Troy Trojans in 1880 as a lefty third baseman, offering proof to future generations why southpaws shouldn't play the hot corner by committing 60 errors in 83 games as a rookie. But he hit .332 and reappeared on the other side of the diamond the following year. Ironically, Connor never led the National League in home runs. He did lead twice in the power stat of the day—triples—and was the 1885 batting champ (.371). His lone home run title came in the only year of the Players' League in 1890. Even if you're inclined to throw out his 14 home runs that year, Connor still had enough to surpass George Stovey's 122, which was set in the American Association and NL in the 1880s. Forgotten today and ignored by the Hall of Fame until eighty-one years after his final game, Connor held the home run title from 1895 until 1921, when a kid named Babe Ruth shattered it for all time.

Tater

Gobbled up by sluggers, loathed by pitchers, a tater is a home run. Though the term had its origins in the Negro Leagues four decades earlier—author Paul Dickson says it may have been for potato or long potato—the colorful 1970s slugger George "Boomer" Scott of the Red Sox and Brewers took to calling his many homers by this moniker. Other home run slang includes big fly, blast, bomb, dinger, donger, four bagger, going yard, jack, and long ball, among other titular titles.

author of thirty-plus books on the Red Sox, have the last word about Fenway's friendliness to hitters. It's a bit of a surprise. "The lack of foul territory—more than any other feature of Fenway—makes it a difficult park for pitchers."

QUOTABLE

The Great Green Equalizer

"The Wall giveth and the Wall taketh away."
—Roger Angell, writer

WHY DOES ST. LOUIS
CARDINALS MANAGER
TONY LaRUSSA
SOMETIMES BAT THE
PITCHER EIGHTH?

he tempting but unsatisfactory answer is simple: Because he's Tony LaRussa. But the argument goes beyond just the manager and arguments can be made on both sides.

Right off the bat, let's just say that some pitchers really can hit. Amateur pitchers, who in many cases are the best athletes on their teams, often bat in the middle of the order. When they turn professional, however, their offensive impact pales in comparison to the importance of their primary task—getting hitters out. Pitching is their job. A select few major league pitchers really are better hitters than the everyday players directly in front of them in the lineup.

Babe Ruth is sort of the ringer in this subset. Yet as a Red Sox pitcher he often batted ninth before his conversion to full-time outfielder. The Babe batted ninth in the 1918 World Series opener, but he hit sixth in Game 4, banged a two-run triple, and picked up the win against the Cubs. Fast-forward several decades . . . Dontrelle Willis, 22-game winner and .261 hitter for the 2005 Marlins, batted seventh and eighth in his starts to boost manager Jack McKeon's depleted Marlins lineup at the end of the season. The 74-year-old McKeon was pondering retirement and D-Train, though prone to wildness on the mound, really could hit.

Other than a few such rare circumstances, professional pitchers usually bat ninth because they can't hit. And then there's the tradition standpoint, which can never be discounted in baseball. It's tough bucking ingrained trends in a game that's been closely followed since the Civil War. John McGraw's pitchers batted ninth, so did Connie Mack's, and Joe McCarthy's, and Casey Stengel's, and Earl Weaver's . . . until the American League adopted the designated hitter rule in 1973. The AL essentially said that pitchers are such bad hitters we're taking them out of the batting order entirely and putting in a real hitter instead.

So in the National League—and for American League teams on the road during interleague and World Series play—the pitcher bats last. Why would he bat anywhere else? But a man making out an unconventional lineup card isn't afraid to tinker with tradition.

Tony LaRussa has been one of the game's top managers since he took over the White Sox in 1979. He guided Chicago to its first postseason appearance in twenty-four years in 1983; he went to Oakland and won four division titles, not to mention three pennants in a row (1988–90) and a world championship; he captured seven more division titles and another World Series after going to St. Louis in 1996. Dave Duncan, a former catcher and LaRussa's teammate with the A's in the late 1960s and early 1970s, took over as LaRussa's pitching coach in 1983 and has remained with him at all his stops. The two are credited—or blamed, depending on your perspective—for forging the era of specialist relief pitching: lefties or righties coming in to face one batter and then departing regardless of result, plus the use of the closer specifically to start the ninth inning and usually only in save situations. Dennis Eckersley became a Hall of Fame closer under this system and made the strategy look like genius. LaRussa, a four-time Manager of the Year, stands second on the all-time list in games managed (4,934 through 2010), trailing only Connie Mack (7,755 games over 53 seasons).

That's a pretty full plate for one career even before altering the one fundamental truth of a National League batting order. His logic— LaRussa is also a lawyer—is that when he has a truly dynamic batter on his team, it is advantageous to the lineup to have the pitcher bat one spot higher so—assuming his pitcher at the plate makes the final out each time—his slugger in the three spot actually serves as the cleanup hitter in every inning he comes to bat except the first. LaRussa first started the practice during Mark McGwire's monster 1998 season. (We won't raise another argument, but it should be noted that McGwire, hired by LaRussa to be hitting coach in St. Louis in 2010, admitted he took steroids during his 70-homer season in '98 and LaRussa, who also managed him in Oakland, has long been Big Mac's biggest defender and apologist.) Starting in 2009, LaRussa again began batting the pitcher eighth regularly as a perceived benefit for Albert Pujols.

Statisticians have said there is some merit to the theory and batting the pitcher eighth can add two runs or more per year to an offense. But batting the pitcher a spot higher than normal can also kill rallies. Say it's the second inning and the five, six, and seven hitters all reach base with no one out—here comes the pitcher up to bat. It's too early to pinch hit and you're offering the opponent a chance to escape a major jam if he retires the .150 eighth hitter and gets the .250 ninth place hitter to bang into a double play. If the lineup is set up the traditional way, the .250 hitter has a better chance of starting a big inning or at least getting a run in—even if he hits into that double play—as opposed to offering the opposition a chance to escape the jam unscathed.

LaRussa sees things differently. "When it happens later in the game you can pinch hit for them," LaRussa explained in 2008. "If he makes an out, Albert's the cleanup hitter. We leave the bases loaded with position players, too."

LaRussa feels the strategy works best if he has a speedy hitter batting ninth, essentially giving him two leadoff hitters. That was his preference during his best years managing Oakland, where he didn't need to worry about the pitcher hitting at all. Ned Yost tried hitting Brewers pitchers eighth on a limited basis in 2008—before he was fired—and John Russell briefly experimented with it for the Pirates—who gave him the ax in 2010. Neither

A 2010 boxscore with the Cardinals' starting pitcher, in this case Blake Hawksworth, batting eighth.

Mets 4, Cardinals 0

St. Louis	AB	R	H	BI	BB	SO	Avg.
F.Lopez 3b	4	0	0	0	0	1	.268
Jay cf	3	0	1	0	0	1	0	.383
Pujols 1b	4	0	0	0	0	1	.295
Holliday lf	4	0	0	0	0	1	.302
Ludwick rf	3	0	1	0	0	0	.279
Schumaker 2b	3	0	1	0	0	0	.261
Y.Molina c	3	0	0	0	0	0	.234
Hawksworth p	2	0	0	0	0	0	.000
D.Reyes p	0	0	0	0	0	0	.000
a-Winn ph	1	0	0	0	0	0	.266
MacDougal p	0	0	0	0	0	0	---
Greene ss	1	0	0	0	1	0	.265
b-Rasmus ph	1	0	1	0	0	0	.271
Totals	29	0	4	0	2	3	

New York	AB	R	H	BI	BB	SO	Avg.
Jos.Reyes ss	5	1	1	0	0	1	.280
Pagan lf	3	2	2	0	1	0	.309
Beltran cf	4	0	1	1	0	0	.229
I.Davis 1b	4	1	1	3	0	0	.252
Hessman 3b	2	0	1	0	1	0	.207
Thole c	2	0	1	0	2	0	.359
Francoeur rf	4	0	0	0	0	1	.241
Cora 2b	3	0	0	0	1	0	.207
Dickey p	4	0	0	0	0	1	.200
F.Rodriguez p	0	0	0	0	0	0	---
Totals	31	4	7	4	5	3	

St. Louis	000	000	000—	0	4	1
New York	003	010	00x—	4	7	0

a-grounded out for D.Reyes in the 8th. b-singled for Greene in the 9th.
E—Greene (5). LOB—St. Louis 4, New York 9. 2B—Jay (12), Jos.Reyes (18). 3B—Pagan (7). HR—I.Davis (15), off Hawksworth. RBIs—Beltran (4), I.Davis 3 (52).
Runners left in scoring position—St. Louis 3 (Holliday 2, Winn); New York 3 (Dickey, Jos.Reyes 2).
Runners moved up—F.Lopez. GIDP—F.Lopez, Schumaker.
DP—New York 2 (I.Davis, Jos.Reyes, Dickey), (I.Davis, Jos.Reyes, I.Davis).

St. Louis	IP	H	R	ER	BB	SO	NP	ERA
Hkswrth L, 4-7	6	7	4	4	3	3	94	5.30
D.Reyes	1	0	0	0	0	0	18	3.14
MacDougal	1	0	0	0	2	0	22	0.00

New York	IP	H	R	ER	BB	SO	NP	ERA
Dickey W, 7-4	8⅓	4	0	0	2	2	118	2.32
Rdrgz S, 22-27	⅔	0	0	0	0	1	6	2.44

Inherited runners-scored—F.Rodriguez 2-0. HBP—by MacDougal (Hessman). WP—Dickey.
Umpires—Home, D.J. Reyburn; First, Jim Wolf; Second, Marvin Hudson; Third, Derryl Cousins.
T—2:26. A—40,087 (41,800).

Walk-off

This refers to players on the visiting team walking off the field after a game-ending hit (or walk, balk, error, sacrifice, wild pitch, hit batter, fielder's choice). Besides having to endure the cheers of the frenzied home crowd, the visitors also have to witness the prolonged celebrations that have become so involved and intense that Angels first baseman Kendry Morales broke his leg and was finished for the year when a walk-off celebration got too extreme in 2010. Players rounding the bases on a walk-off home run usually toss their helmet so as not to get their heads hurt by all the celebratory head pats. Walk-off has become a common term in baseball over the last two decades and was started, ironically, by a player whose job was to prevent walk-off moments: Oakland Hall of Fame closer Dennis Eckersley, who allowed one of the most famous walk-off home runs to Kirk Gibson in the 1988 World Series.

PHOTO CREDIT:
SHUTTERSTOCK IMAGES

skipper has ever been confused with John McGraw or Casey Stengel, managing greats passed by LaRussa in terms of longevity.

So at the end of the day, hitting the pitcher eighth is another of the manager's unique strategies that he values despite the doubts of others. Specialized relief pitching was scoffed at until everyone started copying it.

Amen

"Baseball is like church. Many attend but few understand."
—Wes Westrum, manager

The pitcher batting eighth is a little like a double-switch that moves the pitcher around in the batting order. LaRussa just starts the game with the lineup that way. You wonder what Connie Mack, a proponent of the DH decades before it was enacted, would say about all this.

Some pitchers just look good with a bat in their hands. Pedro Martinez, who last pitched for the 2009 Phillies, spent 18 seasons in the majors and drove in 18 runs while batting .099. Yet in his peak decade (1996 2005) batters hit better than .220 off Pedro only once.

PHOTO CREDIT: DAN CARUBIA

WHAT IS THE MOST MEMORABLE STADIUM PROMOTION EVER HELD?

For many years, owners considered it enough of a promotion to hang a sign outside the ballpark: GAME TODAY, 3 PM. When entertainment choices exploded after World War II and television made sitting at home a lot more appealing to many folks, owners had to start thinking of more ways to get the public's attention—and money.

There have been thousands of different giveaways at major league ballparks (minor league parks have tried yet more schemes, many worthy of an *I Love Lucy* episode). Space forbids us to list these countless clever promotions, so here are five of the most memorable from the major league level—from the doggone fun to the downright dangerous.

Banner Day

There was no worse team in the twentieth century than the 40–120 expansion Mets of 1962, yet after four seasons without National League baseball in New York, people weren't picky. In fact, fans loved Casey Stengel's club so much they wrote their feelings on bed sheets and paraded them through the ancient Polo Grounds in the team's inaugural season. Club policy was to remove them. But Mets president George Weiss, who came from the staid Yankees, was eventually convinced that these fans weren't causing a nuisance, they were causing a phenomenon. The Mets stopped confiscating banners and in 1963 began a unique tradition of inviting fans onto the field to parade their banners (or placards, as Casey called them) between games of a doubleheader, with the best banners earning prizes from a panel of judges. This signature Mets promotion moved with the club to Shea Stadium and continued through 1996. Even if it wasn't a banner year, the Mets and their fans were at least assured of a banner day.

Turn Back the Clock Day

For those who love seeing modern players in old uniforms, it all started with a makeup game caused by a lockout that postponed the start of the 1990 season. The day after the All-Star Game, July 11, the Brewers and White Sox took the field during the final season of original Comiskey Park. The Brewers wore their usual road uniforms, but the White Sox donned replica duds of the club's last world championship team in 1917. Given that the game was held at the same park that the 1917 world champs—and the 1919 Black Sox—called home, it looked like they were filming a prequel or sequel to recent Joe Jackson homage films *Eight Men Out* and *Field of Dreams*. The 40,000 fans at the Wednesday matinee got into the act with grandstand admission for 50 cents and popcorn for a nickel. (Taking note of what happened in Cleveland 16 years earlier, beer was kept at regular price.) Turn Back the Clock would be embraced by many clubs over the next two decades, a nice legacy for old Comiskey.

Grandstand Manager's Day

St. Louis Browns owner Bill Veeck Jr.'s most famous scheme was sending 3-foot-7-inch Eddie Gaedel to pinch hit in August 1951 (he walked!) but later that week Veeck had an even more ingenious plan— Grandstand Manager's Day. Fans sending in a newspaper form that allowed them to set the lineup for the last-place Browns against the almost as lowly Athletics got free admission to the special Grandstand Managers Section at Sportsman's Park. When a decision needed to be made, a sign was raised over the Browns dugout asking what the Browns should do next and 1,115 "managers" responded by holding up color coded cards. Managing by committee resulted in an inning-ending double play after the grandstanders voted to play the infield back. The fans chose to hold off on a hit-and-run with a slow runner and a full count—the batter fanned. The fans were wrong on a later steal attempt, but the Browns ended a four-game losing streak with a 5–3 win. All the while, manager Zach Taylor sat in a rocking chair, smoking a pipe—after all, it was his night off.

Did You Know?

A Baseball Recipe

Though an official major league baseball can be purchased for about $13, the homemade variety is worth a try. Be careful it doesn't burn!

Start with a round cork center (1/2 ounce, 2.86 to 2.94 inches circumference).

Cover with one layer black rubber, then one layer red rubber (7/8 ounce each).

Find 121 yards four-ply gray wool. Wrap vigorously around cork.

Cover with 45 yards of three-ply white wool.

Follow with 53 yards of three-ply grey wool yarn.

Wrap with 150 yards of cotton yarn.

Seal with a layer of rubber cement. (Mind your fingers!)

Take cowhide (horsehide, if you're in a pinch) and fit over ball.

Sew cover together with red cotton yarn lacing thread.

Be sure to use 108 stitches. No more. No less.

It's done when it measures between 9 and 9 1/4 inches and weighs 5 to 5 1/4 ounces.

Voila! Use pitcher to serve.

Disco Demolition Night

If we praise Bill Veeck's ingenuity, he should also be lambasted for his recklessness. Disco Demolition Night was cooked up by a

Chicago disc jockey and set up by Bill's son Mike, who survived the screw-up to have a long career in baseball promotions (though some would argue that there is merit to a promotion still being discussed three decades later). White Sox owner Bill Veeck bared the brunt of blame for signing off on the concept, which was held between games of a July 1979 twi-night doubleheader with the Tigers. Fans were supposed to deposit their detested disco records in a box to be detonated in center field. After the explosion, the packed Comiskey Park crowd continued firing records from the stands and they followed the vinyl onto the field as a riot ensued. The fans would not leave and the players could not return, resulting in a forfeit of the second game of the twinbill and the most ill-fated of Veeck's countless schemes.

Ten-Cent Beer Night

When it comes to on-field riots, no promotion holds a candle to Cleveland's Ten-Cent Beer Night in 1974. Fans at Municipal Stadium could buy as much beer as they liked for a dime a cup, getting about eight beers for the price of one. If the game had been a rout, a riot might have been avoided, but a team without a pennant since 1948

QUOTABLE

Come on Down

"I would love to have a guy that always gets the key hit, a pitcher that always makes his best pitch and a manager that can always make the right decision. The problem is getting him to put down his beer, come out of the stands, and do those things." —Danny Murtaugh, manager.

picked a bad night for a ninth-inning rally. The Rangers bullpen had to be evacuated for safety, fights broke out all over the stands, and fireworks were continually thrown on the field—but to get an idea of how bad things were, consider that the riot was started by a sacrifice fly. As the tying run crossed the plate on John Lowenstein's fly ball, hundreds of fans stormed the field. The Rangers armed themselves with bats and still needed the help of the police and the Indians to escape. Future Hall of Fame umpire Nestor Chylak was hit on the head and Cleveland Indians pitcher Tom Hilgendorf was slammed by a steel chair. And it could have been even worse if the 80,000-seat stadium had been more than quarter full. Though the Indians were in third place at the time—and were practically giving away beer—the Tribe drew just over 23,000 for the Tuesday night tilt, which ended with the Indians forfeiting and a six-pack of fans arrested. With beer back at full price the next night, Cleveland beat the Rangers—in a game this time—in front of 8,101.

"The Mistake by the Lake," Municipal Stadium in Cleveland, in less riotous days. Lord knows how many poles the patrons were seeing on Ten-Cent Beer Night on June 4, 1974.